A Minor Addict

(Based on a true story)

Clay Cassidy

Edited and Published by Clay Cassidy

Also by Clay Cassidy

Payback
The Judge
The Return
The Serial Killer
A Dozen Lawmen
Wrong Diagnosis
Rebel Cowgirl
A Minor Addict
A Dish Best Served Cold

DEDICATION

I dedicate the writing of this novel to all those desperate parents who have children or siblings addicted to dangerous and illegal substances. Thousands of lives are lost daily due to the misuse of these illegal substances supplied by dealers who have no remorse getting people, young and old, hooked to a life of sorrow.

Content

ACKNOWLEDGMENTS

I'd like to thank the Drug Counselling Centre for the information which they supplied concerning the addiction and treatment of addictive substances, and then to Dr's R.C Malenka, E.J. Nestler, and S.E. Hyman (2009), Chapter 15: "Reinforcement and Addictive Disorders", Neuropharmacology: Foundation for Clinical Neuroscience (2nd Edition).Methamphetamine. PubChem Compound, and the National Center for Biotechnology.

i

Prologue

She can't stand by herself, and has to hold onto a nearby pole. Clark gazes in bewilderment at the three of them as they pass the joint around, taking turns to drag on it. The women, who have been keeping watch while their children play in the park, hastily depart now.

Clark shakes his head and says "I'm not staying here any longer, Shelley. You ought to be ashamed of yourself for smoking an unlawful substance. You're still a minor on top of it all."

Shelley giggles while she replies "Clark, don't be such a ninny, it's only a little weed, and it's not like I'm addicted to the stuff, you know. I won't do it again, I promise. John, Lilly, in future you shouldn't smoke in my presence, okay? There, are you satisfied now Clark?"

Chapter One

2 December 2006; 16H00. Shelley stares out of the car window as it speeds onwards on the busy highway. She is extremely beautiful and each feature compliments the other. Her face is heart-shaped with a cleft in the middle of her chin and full, voluptuous lips. Her complexion is sallow.

Shelley's nose is perfectly straight and she has beautiful dark brown, Almond-shaped eyes with long lashes. Her long, dark-brown hair is naturally curly, and almost reaches her waist.

It's summer time, and the family is on their way to spend the holidays at the coast. Between all the kempt-up excitement Shelley is not in the least bit happy about her parents' plans once they return home.

Shelley is only thirteen and in grade eight. She feels very vulnerable at this stage of her life, both emotionally and psychologically. Everything is changing and happening so rapidly at this precise time in her life. There's Mike, her first love, whom she adores to death with his handsome baby face and blue eyes. Shelley is crying softly, and wishes she is able to speak to Mike right at this moment. She is sure he will tell her that everything is going to be alright.

During her Primary school years, Shelley is a popular student in all her classes, lively and full of mischief. She excels at school though, and as reward for her hard work, receives an Academic Award at the end of Grade 7. As the best student in English in her Grade, she walks away with the Floating trophy that year. Since then, a whole year has elapsed, and everything has changed so rapidly and irrevocably permanent.

Shelley can feel that she has changed, or rather, matured a little. This "maturity" brings about other problems that her father, Nick, doesn't approve of at all. One of them is the frequent visiting of boys at their home.

Nick Callahan is as Irish as they come. Short- tempered and a man of few words, he stands five feet eleven inches tall; definitely a man to be reckoned with. Naturally muscular in build, and having had his fair share of skirmishes while growing up, he can handle himself very well.

He too has a sallow complexion, with curly black hair and green eyes; strong facial features with a wide jaw that gives him character. Shelley is aware that her father has looked at her in the rear-view mirror once or twice during their trip to the Airport Hotel, but he doesn't say anything when he sees her crying.

They arrive at their destination, where they will spend the night, and board the Airplane early the following morning to fly to the coast. Shelley wipes her face with a cloth that Constance, her mother, hands to her, aware of her daughter's distressing circumstances.

Constance is Nick's first love. He is smitten with her the moment he meets her, and falls completely and utterly in love. In fact; it is love at first sight for both of them. She is a very beautiful woman, with a fair complexion, soft, full lips, and blue-green eyes with perfect white teeth.

Her black hair is thick and straight, and falls to her shoulders. Constance is soft and caring, pouring out her love on her children and Nick. She also just as quickly turns into a Tigress if she becomes aware that either of her children or husband are being threatened, and will fight to the death to protect them.

All this time, Clark, who is Shelley's older brother, is content with whatever happens. Clark is nearly three years Shelley's senior, and an exact copy of Nick, except that they don't share the same temper. Clark is softhearted like Constance, and has a gentle nature.

Besides his good nature, Clark is a true leader, and not a pushover. He's never been persuaded to do anything against his will, even if it means not being accepted by others. Clark likes being at home, either watching television or listening to music on his hi-fi stereo system. He too has black hair, with only a slight kink in it. He is about to start his first job in the New Year.

"Good afternoon and welcome to our Hotel; Madam, Sir."

This is the Head porter who welcomes the Callahan-family as they arrive as guests of the Hotel. Checking in takes approximately twenty minutes. Nick has to fill out forms and pay in advance for the evening's stay in the Hotel.

Shelley is in awe with surroundings in the foyer, and cocktail drinks and an assortment of cold treats are being served to all the arriving guests. The children receive soft drinks. The front- desk Manager turns his attention to Nick.

"Where can my Porter collect your baggage, mister Callahan? If you could please just send someone with him, he will deliver your suitcases to your Hotel room. Here is your electronic card to open the door to your suite, room number 218. I wish you a pleasant stay, and should you need anything from the kitchen at all, just dial a nine, and you'll be directly connected to the kitchen."

Nick Callahan nods his head at the manager and turns to Clark when he says "Thank you. Clark, will you please accompany the Porter to where we've parked the car? Just open the trunk for him and come right on back; you don't have to wait there."

"Sure dad, no problem. Be back in a jiffy."

Without any further ado, Clark takes the keys from Nick and summonses the Porter to follow him. Nick turns around to speak to Constance, but finds that he is standing alone. His eyes search the foyer and he sees that the two of them are walking towards a boutique to look at the clothes on display.

Nick decides to have something to eat and pour himself some juice while the ladies enjoy a little sightseeing of their own. They will be in the Hotel suite the whole night, because Nick has thought of ordering their dinner from room service instead of going down to the Restaurant to dine.

With Clark and Shelley in tow, Nick and Constance follow the Porter to the lifts. He pushes the button for the second floor. Within a couple of minute's the Callahan's are standing in their suite. Nick tips the Porter and he departs.

It's already early evening and Nick says "Alright everybody, decide what you'd like to eat and drink for dinner, and we'll have some room service."

While waiting for Constance and the children to decide, Nick dials the front desk. A lady answers and Nick puts in their orders for dinner.

Dinner arrives at seven thirty. After a hearty meal, a little television and a welcome cup of coffee, everybody is ready to get a good night's sleep. Four o'clock isn't very far off.

xxx

December 3, 2006, 04:15AM.

The Callahan's get ready to go downstairs for the shuttle that leaves for the Airport at half past four. The ride to the Airport in the shuttle is quick and quiet, as everybody is still a bit woozy from sleeping only five hours.

After the shuttle drops the Callahan's off at the airport, things start running a little smoother. They check in and wait in queue to board the plane. Their flight is delayed for almost an hour, and at quarter to seven, everybody is allowed to board. Constance has a fear of flying, and does not want to be seated close to the window. She takes an aisle-seat instead.

Forty minutes of flying brings them to their destination at the North coast International Airport, and after a twenty-minute wait, Nick and Clark collect their luggage before walking over to the car hire agency just across from the Airport exit. Their car is ready at their arrival, and putting their luggage in the boot, they take the road to the South coast.

Shelley is first to break the silence in the car when she says, "Daddy, do we really have to move after the holiday? All my friends are there, and Mike as well. I can't start all over and make new friends again. Besides, what about me and Mike; don't you care about our feelings?"

"Shelley, mom and I have explained the situation to you. There is no other alternative at this point. If something else should happen to come along, we'll reconsider our options. Whining isn't going to get you anywhere. Be positive about it and something good might just come of it. Tell you what. Would you like a new cell phone, both you and Clark? I'll buy you each one as soon as we arrive at our destination. Is that a deal?"

Shelley looks up and into the rear view mirror, straight into Nicks eyes. She sees the lines around Nick's eyes, and knows that he is smiling at her. Suddenly she feeels like a scoundrel. Wiping her tears, and giving Nick her bravest of smiles, she nods her head.

"Thank you, daddy. That is so considerate of you. I appreciate it, but I don't want you to think that it's going to change my opinion."

"No, of course not, sweetie. It's not an offer to bribe you, it's just that I've been aware that you have no way of contacting your friends when you want to. This will enable you to constact them when and where you like. Clark, I know your cell phone's outdated, so you're also getting a new one, okay?"

"That's awesome, thanks, dad."

Clark smiles from ear to ear. Constance leans over and squeezes Shelley's hand, smiling at her and Clark. She likes seeing them happy, and loves Nick for doing just that. Leaning over, she kisses Nick on the cheek.

"Thank you, lover boy", she says with an enchanting smile on her lips.

"What did I do?", Nick asks surprised

"You've given the kids something to look forward to. You know how happy it makes me, and I hate seeing Shelley so heart-broken. I think you've managed to make her forget home for a while."

Nick turns his head and looks at Constance, smiling at her.

"That's fine my girl; no sweat. Anything in particular you'd like; besides me, that is?"

Constance lifts her eyebrows, laughing in mockery at Nick's question. Clark and Shelley join in the laughter, and without a doubt Nick knows that this is going to be a holiday to remember forever.

It's nearly 10 AM, and they are nearing the off- ramp which will take them to their holiday destination. The sea has been visible now for quite some time, which makes the conversation and spirit light-hearted and very amiable.

"Ah, here we go kids; the off ramp's just in front. Another five kilometers, and we'll be there. Once we've unpacked, we can go and have a look at what's where. Let's make a day of it, and ride out to a larger beach, what do you say?"

Constance shakes her head, making another suggestion instead.

"Baby, let's rather go tomorrow. I think we're all tired from getting up very early, flying to the coast, and driving another hour and a half to get here. I'd suggest we take it calm today, rest out and get everything in order at the holiday home first. Besides, we have to go and get a few things if you guys want something to eat or drink a little later on."

There are murmurs of confirmation and acceptance at this suggestion from Constance, which makes Nick realize that he too, is a little bushed, and would rather welcome a little afternoon nap. He tells Constance of his plan, and she just smiles at him, knowing that the suggestion he's made, is only to please the children.

Then they're at their destination, the house looming up in front of them. Shelley and Clark each choose the rooms they like best, and after enjoying a light but wholesome lunch, everybody goes upstairs and unpacks. At two thirty the house is silent; the Callahan's are taking a well-deserved afternoon nap.

A MINOR ADDICT

The vacation is spectacular, and Nick and Constance spare no expense. They all have a wonderful time, and Shelley even manages to forget about the problems that she was so upset about beforehand. Arriving home brings back all Shelley's concerns and heartache within a couple of days.

Both she and Mike seem to take the relocation to the city extremely hard, although it will still be another six months down the line before any plans will be set into motion. Fortunately, they both seem to find solace in this fact.

The following six months seem to sprout wings, for almost overnight it's time to take leave of the place which the Callahan's had called home for so many years, especially the children. Shelley is affected most by all of the changes happening so quickly.

She's been crying her eyes out for the last couple of days, having to leave behind all her friends she's had since starting pre-school. Fortunately, she and Mike separated earlier on in the year, so it's one problem less to worry about.

Clark resigns from his job, hoping to find a better opportunity in the city. Nick's new job will be a welcome challenge to him, and Constance; well, she just looks forward to a change of scenery, although Nick knows that she will enjoy shopping at the Malls. It's going to be the beginning of a new chapter in their lives.

CHAPTER TWO

———

March 2008-an upmarket estate somewhere close to the city.

Clark and Shelley enjoy the freedom inside the Estate brought about by Security access control to the Estates' entrance. Clark and Shelley are visiting with two of Shelley's friends in the Estate's park. A couple of toddlers are playing in the sandpits, with their mothers entertaining them. Clark is not happy, for Shelley and her two friends are smoking weed; an illegal substance. Clark is usually quiet and minds his own business, but he decides to speak up and keep Shelley in check.

* Marijuana, also known as weed, Ganja, Dope, Grass, Green, Hash, Joint, Mary Jane(MJ), Loud, Blunt, Skunk, Pot, Sinsemilla. It is the most widely used illegal drug in the world, and a product of the hemp plant Cannabis Sativa. The main active chemical in this drug, also present in other forms of cannabis, is THC (delta-9-tetrahydrocannabinol).

Of the nearly 400 chemicals found in the plant, THC affects the brain the most. This drug is a green or grey mixture of dried, shredded flowers and leaves of the hemp plant, Cannabis Sativa. Users roll loose weed into cigarettes called a "joint."

It can also be smoked in a pipe or water pipe called a "bong", or vaporized using a "vape" pen. A single inhalation of smoke from a joint is called a "hit." The drug can also be mixed into food or brewed as tea and ingested, and has appeared in cigars called "blunts." It also comes in the form of a wax which resembles lip balm that can be eaten or smoked.

Marijuana, or weed, as it is more commonly known, has short and long term effects on users, which are very bad for health. The short term effects are disrupted learning and memory, difficulty with thinking and problem solving, distorted perception(sight, sounds, time, touch), loss of motor coordination, increased heart rate, and anxiety. These effects are even greater when used together with something like alcohol. A dry mouth will also be experienced in most cases.

Long term effects of Marijuana (Weed) includes the following. It increases the risk of chronic cough, Bronchitis, and increases the risk of schizophrenia in people who are vulnerable individuals. It also increases the risk of anxiety, depression and a series of attitude and personality changes also known as "amotivational syndrome."

This syndrome is characterized by a diminished ability to carry out long-term plans, a sense of apathy, decreased attention to appearance and behavior, as well as decreased ability of concentration for long periods of time.

"Shelley, what do you think you're doing? Mom will have a fit, and dad's going to roast your backside. You know what they said about taking addictive substances."

A feeling of desperation descends over Clark. How is he going to explain this to their parents? Clark feels responsible for Shelley although he knows that she will never listen to him. Taking the self-rolled, foul-smelling joint, Shelley laughs at Clark while holding her arm stretched out towards him.

"C'mon Clark, take a drag. Stop being such a spoilsport; get a life. You'll see; it's fun."

Shelley takes a long drag, inhaling the smoke deep into her lungs. Her friends laugh and dare her to take another. Shelley's face becomes ashen, and Clark sees the drug take effect on Shelley. She starts giggling uncontrollably, and struggles to get up, losing her balance in the process.

She is unable to stand by herself, and has to hold onto a nearby pole. Clark gazes in bewilderment at the three of them as they pass the joint around, taking turns to drag on it. The women, who have been playing in the park with their children, hastily start to depart.

"I'm not staying here any longer, Shelley. You ought to be ashamed of yourself for smoking an unlawful substance. You're still a minor on top of it all."

"Clark, don't be such a ninny, it's only a little weed, and it's not like I'm addicted to the stuff, you know. I won't do it again, I promise. John, Lilly, in future you shouldn't smoke in my presence, okay? There, are you satisfied now, Clark?"

Both John and Lilly look with open disgust at Clark.

"As long as you don't tell your parents that we gave her the weed to smoke, I don't have any beef, Clark", John says, his speech a little slurry.

Shelley's pupils are dilated, and her eyes are fixed and unresponsive. Clark can see that Shelley is in a world of her own.

Clark helps her up and takes her to a nearby tap, where he helps her drink some water. He also splashes water in her face. Shelley looks a little better, although the effects of the weed have still not worn off.

Her eyes can still not focus, and she complains about nausea. Clark decides that it's time to return home before their father gets back. If he sees Shelley in this condition, there will definitely be trouble.

They are close to the town house where they live, and with a sickening feeling, Clark sees that his father's car is in the garage. He waits for Shelley to catch up with him, but she waves for him to carry on.

"Go on ahead Clark. I'll be there shortly; I just need to get some more fresh air."

Without waiting for Shelley, Clark goes on ahead and enters the house.

"Hi dad, hi mom; I'm home. Shelley's on her way."

Nick looks up from the newspaper he's reading.

"Hey Clark, what've you and your sister been up to today?"

"Nothing much, dad. How was your day at work?"

There's a commotion outside, and Constance looks questioningly at Clark when they hear Shelley cuss and then giggle.

"Oh, hell. Dad, I promise Shelley didn't want to listen to me. She, she …"

Shelley enters with a bang, sprawling on the tile floor. Still giggling, she cautiously gets to her feet and tries to find her balance. She cusses again.

"These damn shoes, I'm going to break my neck with them. Oh, hi everybody!"

Clark hears his mother inhale sharply.

"You'd better watch your language, young lady! What's wrong with you; have you been drinking? Nick?"

Nick himself is shocked by Shelley's unfavorable behavior, and is speechless for a moment or two, but quickly finds his footing again.

"Come here, Shelley."

Shelley allows Nick to smell her breath at his request. Nick shakes his head as he looks at Constance and says "She hasn't been drinking, my dear. Where are you going Clark? Come back here, and tell us what your sister's been up to. You were with her, so you ought to know what she did. Please don't lie to us. Let's see, her pupils are dilated, she's giggling uncontrollably, and she doesn't seem to have any balance. I also smell a strange odor on her breath I don't know. It's not cigarette smoke …"

"Oh no! Clark? Where did she get hold of whatever it is she took?"

Looking at Clark, it's obvious to Nick that their son is shaken by the matter.

"Dad, mom, I tried talking to her, but she just wouldn't listen. Shelley and two of her friends were smoking weed in the park."

Clark's face is ash-white with fright. Nick indicates to Clark to sit down.

"It's okay son, we're not mad at you. We just want to know what happened, and Shelley's old enough to take the blame for her own wrong doings. You're not to blame for her mistakes, and we want you to remember that."

"Thanks dad, you don't know what a relief that is."

In the meantime, Shelley wonders off into the kitchen and opens the refrigerator. She takes out some leftover roast from the previous evening's dinner. Constance throws her hands in the air.

"Now she has the munchies! What are we going to do, Nick? No wonder her grades have taken a turn for the worst, and her attitude just stinks, to say the least. The "friends" she hangs out with are all deadbeats. There has to be something we can do!"

Nick looks at Shelley for some time before answering his wife's question. His eyes are sad as he frowns.

"I have no idea what we're going to do, my girl. I will tell you this, though She is grounded until she has proven to us that she can act responsibly and grown-up, and has changed her ways. She goes to school and back, and she is not to have any visits from friends, I don't care what the excuse might be. Oh, that guy who has been coming around to visit; I'll sort him out myself. His days of visiting Shelley are over. He's much too old for her anyway, and besides, I don't trust him."

Shelley saunters closer, still eating, and hears this last remark of Nick's. With a scowl on her face, she takes a stance right in front of her father, and tries looking him squarely in the eye. Shelley's speech is a little slurred when she speaks.

"I will see Lee, dad. He's my boyfriend. If you won't allow me to see him, I'll do it behind your back, and then you'll be sorry!"

"Shelley, have some respect when you talk to your father! I won't tolerate you speaking to him in that tone, do you hear me? What's more; I agree with what your father says, so the sooner you decide to change your ways, the quicker you get to resume a normal life."

"I hate you all! Clark, I'll never forgive you for telling on me, tattle-tale. The best you can do, is get a job and stop hanging around the house all day. You're a lazy bum!"

"That's enough, Shelley! We can all do without the insults. I think it would be better if you go to your room and stay there."

"Yes, mother!"

Shelley stumbles off to confine herself to her room. In her fuzzy brain she is the victim of a plot to drive her insane. She kicks her shoes across the room, and falls down on her bed, allowing the darkness to engulf and pull her into a world where nothingness rules.

A MINOR ADDICT

Very early the following morning.

Shelley doesn't understand why Clark is giving her the cold shoulder, and Constance has spoken but a few words with her. Usually there is a lot of talking around the breakfast table, but this morning is different. She can't place her finger on it, but something gives her the idea that she is to blame for it all. The ride to school is uncomfortable and quiet, and Shelley decides to break the ice by starting up a conversation.

"Daddy, what seems to be the matter this morning? Mom and Clark have been giving me the silent treatment since I woke up this morning, and you don't seem too eager to speak to me either. Did I say or do something to upset someone?"

Nick can't believe what he is hearing. He glances sideways at Shelley, and sees that she has a puzzled expression on her face. Can it be that she doesn't remember anything from the previous day?

"Can't you remember what happened yesterday, Shelley?"

"Well daddy, I remember sitting in the park with Clark and friends of mine, then I woke up and it was morning. That's really all I remember. It feels like I slept for a year. Apart from that I have a headache that's killing me; must be because I slept for so long."

Pulling the car off the road, Nick takes the time to explain to Shelley what happened the previous day. As he talks, Nick sees the tears well up in Shelley's beautiful eyes, and roll down her cheeks. By the time he is finished talking, Shelley is sobbing uncontrollably.

"Oh daddy, I'm so, so sorry! What have I done? I can't bear to look either one of you, including Clark, in the eyes again. Please forgive me? I promise it'll never happen again. I'll behave from now on."

Nick lifts her chin so Shelley faces him.

"Honey, everybody makes mistakes. The main thing is, we have to learn that actions have consequences. Unfortunately, you're going to have to pay the price for being involved with taking an unlawful substance. You're grounded, and until such time that mom and I are satisfied that you've kicked the habit of smoking weed, you won't go anywhere without either one of us being present. As for Lee, he can come over on a Friday night and Saturday afternoon, but there will not be any going out. He'll visit you at home only. It's not negotiable. Those are the terms."

Shelley nods her head.

"It's fine, daddy; thank you. I promise I'll pull myself together from now on. I've also been neglecting my school work, but my grades will pick up to what they were before; promise."

Happy that they've had the chance to talk about things, Nick drops Shelley off at school and returns home to get his lunch for work. While getting his things together, Nick quickly tells Constance of the latest developments, and what he's decided. Constance is happy that things have turned out the way they did. With a mended heart, she goes about her daily tasks.

A MINOR ADDICT

Thursday, April 26, 2008; 10:45PM.

Life in the Callahan household is not as it should be. The situation has been snowballing now for the past three weeks, simmering like a volcano ready to erupt at any time.

Shelley was grounded in March for three weeks, and has been responsive to all the rules. She does her chores as expected of her, and pushes her grades back to where they were. Nick and Constance decide that she can be trusted again, and lift her punishment at the end of March.

Shelley is in seventh heaven, as Lee plans to have a small party at his father's house, and invites only a small group of his friends to the gathering. Shelley asks her parents for permission to join the party. Her parents agree, but there is a condition.

Nick and Constance insist that Clark accompany her, and give them a curfew of 11:30PM. Nick drops them off at Lee's house at seven o'clock, with Lee promising that he'll have Clark and Shelley back home before their curfew.

Nick feels uneasy, but can't exactly pin-point why and, not wanting to pull everything out of proportion, agrees that it will be fine. As promised, both Shelley and Clark arrive home ten minutes earlier than expected, which pleases both Nick and Constance, although Shelley doesn't quite look herself.

Avoiding conversation, Shelley excuses herself, saying that she is tired and wants to get into bed. Without giving either of them a goodnight kiss, she goes to her room and closes the door. Nick, frowning, looks at Constance and, shrugging his shoulders, turns his attention to Clark, whom he subsequently also finds not very talkative. He is in actual fact, a little evasive answering Nick's questions. After some ten minutes, Clark says that he has a headache and is going to bed.

Shelley isn't the same since returning home from the party, and no matter how Constance tries to talk to her, she closes up as tight as a clam. It's as if Shelley has undergone an overnight metamorphosis.

Even on her birthday two weeks later, 12 May 2008, when she turns sixteen, she insists that she wants to go to the movies instead of having a bash at home. Shelley and a couple of her friends, including Lee and Clark, go to the movies to celebrate her sixteenth birthday. Her parents extend her curfew for the occasion.

Nick is suspicious about certain behavioral characteristics of Shelley's. Constance is worried and wants to find out what the problem is, but Nick cautions her to be patient. Nick too, has become aware that Shelley is slipping away from them, but doesn't know why. He doesn't want Constance to know that he is worried, because it will only aggravate the situation further.

A MINOR ADDICT

16 May 2008. There is trouble yet again in the Callahan household.

Nick and Shelley have a difference of opinion, and a hefty quarrel ensues. She goes out on a date with Lee without Nick's permission, and arrives home later than usual. Upon confronting her, Nick comes close enough to smell alcohol on her breath.

He can now understand why she's tried to keep her distance from him, and also why she is so sassy and witty. It is however, not the first time that Shelley has been caught drinking.

"I hate it here; all your rules! The what and what not's! It's only your way, or no way at all. You never take my feelings into consideration! I wish I was eighteen so I could get out and live on my own! I'd rather stay with Lee; he's the only one who understands me!"

Nick is furious but tries to keep calm. He doesn't want the situation to escalate. Shelley is already half hysterical.

"Shelley, calm down. Nobody's trying to keep you locked up in a cage, as you seem to think. Your mother and I are concerned about you, that's all. You've changed, and it's not for the best, that I can assure you. Even your teachers have expressed their concern about the sudden change in your behavior. What's the matter? Talk to us, we're here to help you if you have problems you can't solve."

"Just leave me alone, all of you! I'm sick of you, you hear me; sick! You're not a father's ass!"

Shelley starts laughing hysterically, pointing her finger at Nick. Constance shakes Shelley and retorts "Shelley, stop that! You have no right to speak to your father that way!"

"What would you know, mother? You're pathetic! Can't you make your own decisions; say what you really feel? No, you follow daddy like a mole; eyes completely shut! Don't lecture me. I know what I want from life, and I'll get it too, make or break!"

Nick turns and walks away; he doesn't know how to handle this outburst. Why and when did Shelley develop such hateful thoughts towards them? It's Nick's opinion that someone must be poisoning her mind with her a bunch of crap; there has to be an instigator behind her sudden change of character. Shelley continues to scream at Nick as he makes for the bedroom door.

"Yes, that's good; turn and run. You know I'm right, that's why you don't have anything to say!"

Nick turns around and retraces his steps. He faces Shelley.

"Don't let's say anything we'll regret later, Shelley. I'm not in the mood for putting up a fight with you again tonight."

"You're a chicken daddy. C'mon; admit it! Can't you handle your sixteen-year old daughter?"

Nick's face contorts with rage as Shelley openly continues to taunt him.

"That's better, you look a little revved-up, father! Hit me; hit me! Too scared? I knew you didn't have it in you."

Nick becomes so enraged that he can't think straight, and then it's too late. He strikes Shelley with an open hand. The loud smack echoes in the room as it lands high on her cheekbone.

"Nick, don't!"

In an instant Constance is there, grabbing hold of Nick's arm. She's never before seen him this outraged, but she can also understand why he'd done what he did. Shelley sobs softly and covers her eye with her hand.

Constance takes Shelley's hand away from her face, and is shocked at what she sees. Shelley's left eye is nearly swollen shut, and has a bluish discoloration. The inside of her eye is red, indicating that a vein has burst. Nick is sitting on the bed, holding his head in his hands.

Constance leads Shelley to her own room, and going to the freezer, hurriedly puts ice into a cloth, covering Shelley's eye with it to stop any further swelling. Nick goes to stand in the doorway of Shelley's room and apologizes to her.

"I'm so sorry, Shelley. I didn't mean to strike you."

"Oh daddy, I'm just as sorry. I'm equally to blame; I shouldn't have spoken to you like I did. I don't know why I did it."

Nick and Shelley talk for a little while longer before they decide to call it a night.

xxx

The following morning.

Shelley's eye looks worse than the previous evening. Constance requests of Shelley to stay home until the following Monday, but Shelley refuses.

"Mom, I'll lose too much work at school, and besides, plenty of children go to school with black eyes. I'll just say I fell or something and hit my eye. Don't worry, it'll be alright."

Reassuring both Constance and Nick that she will be alright, Nick drops Shelley off at school, and rides off to start his day. If Nick knew what that day would bring, he'd have reported the incident in case of repercussions later on, and to stop people who knew nothing, from interfering in a case which was sorted out the previous night. Instead, that is not to be, and the scenario is blown completely out of proportion.

A MINOR ADDICT

Friday, May 17 2008-14H50PM.

Nick arrives at the Estate without Shelley. She is not at school when Nick goes to pick her up. Nick waits outside the school for quite some time before he returns home.

He doesn't know what he is going to say to Constance. Nick supposes that Shelley has taken a ride with one of her friends, and hopes that she'll be at home when he gets there.

Arriving home, Nick is surprised to find that Shelley is not there, and that neither Constance nor Clark have heard anything from her. Nick is about to tell Constance about Shelley not showing up after school, when Clark enters the front door.

"Why are the police here, dad? Missus Carmichael and Carmen are with them, as well as Shelley."

Before Nick can reply, two policemen and missus Carmichael come into view, entering through the gate. Nick invites them inside, and looks questioningly from one to the other, a puzzled expression on his face. Missus Carmichael seizes the opportunity to speak first.

"Mister Callahan, I've taken Shelley to see a Doctor and fill out a report to state that she has been assaulted. Photos have been taken at the Police station to verify that fact and a case of assault and battering on a minor has been filed against you. I will be representing Shelley when the case goes to court. She will be taken out of your custody as of today and placed with me until the trial is over. These policemen are here to take a statement from both you and your wife."

Nick's mouth gapes. How can this be happening? Everything was sorted out the previous evening, and even this morning Shelley seemed fine, with no intent on doing anything like this. Nick is the first to find his voice.

"Uhm well, I, I …, we sorted this whole unfortunate business out last night, didn't we Shelley? At least, that's what we were led to believe. Officers, you're welcome to take our statements, but I assure you it's one big misunderstanding."

Shelley never looks at, nor speaks to either one of her parents the entire time Nick's statement is being taken. She takes the opportunity to pack some of her clothes to take with. Clark is shaken by the entire fiasco, and just stares at Shelley. He can't believe that Shelley has stirred up trouble the previous evening, just to have their family-life destroyed in the blink of an eye.

"You're evil Shelley, do you know that? Why are you doing this? Do you want dad to go to jail; what for? You don't have any idea what you're about to let happen, just because you can't adhere to rules in the house, and because Lee's been filling your head with lies that you believe. You're naïve, and I feel sorry for you. Of course, now I'm telling mom and dad everything you've been doing for the last three months. You've been blackmailing me long enough. No more!"

Clark looks at missus Carmichael to see what the impact of his words are, and is relieved to see a look of astonishment on the face of Shelley's friend, as well as on that of missus Carmichael. What they've just heard has shocked them. It has the desired effect that Clark had hoped for. Meanwhile, Constance arranges with missus Carmichael to meet with her and the policemen at her house at seven o'clock that evening to give a statement.

Without even a goodbye or a glimpse in their direction, Shelley gets in the car with the Carmichael's and they drive off. Both Constance and Nick are devastated with the way things have turned out since the previous evening. Nick wishes that he can turn back time just one day.

"Dad, Mom; there's something I would like to get off my chest. It concerns Shelley, and what she's been doing behind your back for the last three months. I've kept quiet, because she's been black-mailing me, and I'm not proud of that. I know now that I should've come to you earlier, but I really didn't think it would go this far, or that Shelley would get so nasty."

"Come and sit down, son, and tell us what's on your mind. Just so you know, we're not holding you accountable for anything that Shelley's done. Like I said before, she's not your responsibility, and you don't owe her anything except love."

"Thanks dad, yeah; I know I don't owe Shelley anything, but she's my little sister, and I feel I have to look out for her, you know? She has this idea that she knows everything, but I've seen first-hand that she has no idea what goes on in life. Neither do I, but I don't even think of doing the things she does. She's been smoking weed ever since that day she did it for the first time in the park. She has never stopped doing it, and I doubt whether she ever will, well, that's to say for as long as she hangs out with Lee. He smokes weed too. You remember that night in April we went to his party? Something happened there that night that I'm ashamed to talk about, or tell you. Lee gave Shelley a lot of alcohol to drink, and she wouldn't pay any attention to my warnings. Then he ... he took her to a flat-let outside and took advantage of her disposition. I went looking for her, and saw everything happening through the window. I was so furious dad, but I couldn't do anything; his brothers were there too. I'm sorry, dad."

There is an intense silence for a couple of minutes while both Nick and Constance try to take in the shocking, disappointing news. Nick feels like his whole world has turned upside down. Constance feels like she's in a whirlpool, and can't find her way back out. Shelley was still under age, so it was Statutory rape!

"I'm going to kill the little shit! Not only did he destroy Shelley's life; he also took her innocence! I knew he was a no good skunk. He's a piece of trash, and now I also know why I never liked nor trusted him. I should've gone with my gut feeling!"

Constance is just as shaken by the entire fiasco but calmer than Nick.

"Nick, calm down, my darling. There's no use in you getting so upset over a piece of trash like him. He's not worth going to jail for. Besides, killing him won't solve our problem with Shelley and the drugs, will it?"

Nick hugs Constance close.

"What would I do without you? Here I am, thinking of revenge, while you're thinking of helping Shelley, even after what she did today. I feel like an idiot, but I still wish he'd die!"

"I understand better than you might think, my darling. You think I don't wish him bad? It's not going to solve our problem, and that's what we have to focus on right now. Shelley is our number one priority."

Shelley's head has been spinning ever since her friend Carmen saw her face and forced the truth from her. After that, she can't seem to remember much, things have happened so fast.

One moment she is still talking, the next they're on their way to a Doctor. She is asked questions; the police interrogate her and take photos.

A MINOR ADDICT

The Doctor gives her injections for the pain and the swelling, and it makes her woozy. She wants to talk to her mom and dad, but her brain is fuzzy from the injection she has received, and she can't focus on what to say.

Shelley feels like a zombie, but at least she now feels better after sleeping a while. She is not going to get her father prosecuted for what has happened, and will tell the detectives so. First of all, she has to speak to missus Carmichael and set things straight. Things have now gone too far.

xxx

17 May 2008, 19H00 PM-The Carmichael residence.

Nick is sitting in the car, waiting for Constance to return. It has been agreed that Nick will not speak to, nor see Shelley, when they arrive at the Carmichael residence that evening. The police want to speak to Constance alone. She has already been inside now for almost forty-five minutes, and Nick wonders what is being said behind the four walls.

Constance looks from Shelley to the two policemen sitting opposite her in missus Carmichael's study, where the interrogation is being held.

"Inspector, Sergeant, this is all a huge misunderstanding, as I'm sure you'll come to see once I've told you all the facts."

"Okay missus Callahan, we're ready to begin. Let's take it from the beginning ..."

"And that gentlemen, is what happened. I'm sure that if any of you has a daughter, you'd react in exactly the same way my husband did."

The Inspector stares at Shelley.

"What do you have to say for yourself, young lady? Think very clearly about the situation and what part you played in it. Then tell me; do you still want your father prosecuted? Be glad you're not my daughter, because I would have had that guy locked up and behind bars right this minute!"

Shelley, in the meantime, gets up and goes to sit on Con-stance's lap. Tears roll down her cheeks as she looks at her mother.

"I'm so sorry about all of this, mom. I didn't mean for it to go this far. I don't want to prosecute daddy."

Shelley looks at the policemen.

"Withdraw the charges please, and close the file."

Missus Carmichael suggests that Shelley spends the night with them, and return home the following day, in order to give everybody some time to adapt to circumstances.

It takes some time for Nick to adjust and put everything behind him, but as time goes by, things in the Callahan household return to normal. There is laughter and joy again.

Security denies Lee any entry into the Estate after Nick supplies them with his vehicle registration number and a photo of him, and warn him to stay away from Shelley, should he wish not to be prosecuted by the law. He takes the easy way out.

Shelley becomes her old self again, and the improvement is monumental. She is daddy's little girl again. Nick still drops her off at school, and picks her up in the afternoon. His work allows him a lot of flexi-hours so he can work in all his other chores without neglecting his job.

This suits everyone in the family, as Nick has time to spend with all of them. Clark lands a job at quite a large Liquor Store, and also works very pleasant hours, with a not too shabby salary. Life is good.

2nd June 2008; an upmarket suburb.

The Callahan's move to a very upmarket suburb. It's a little more expensive, but has all the luxury that comes with the monthly instalment.

Apart from the large four-bedroomed house with two separate dining rooms, a large kitchen and two bathrooms, it also has a two-bedroomed flat and a pleasant-sized swimming pool. To top it off, it has a large yard with a landscaped garden. Constance and the children are ecstatic. Nick has to buy more furniture.

The pool's renovation is paid for by the owner as part of the leasing contract, and is completed just as summer starts. A pool-party is inevitable. With Nick's permission, a small party, which include only a couple of invited guests, is organized for the following Friday night.

Nick makes it clear that anyone who shows up uninvited at the party, will be thrown out and the party will end immediately. These rules accepted, it's a long week until Friday.

The party starts as planned, with only a handful of selected friends known personally to the Callahan's. Everybody enjoys the party, until Nick leaves to get more snacks for the teenagers.

When he returns, there are cars parked everywhere, and music pounds away ridiculously loud somewhere in the yard. Walking around the outside of the house to the back where the pool is, Nick's temper flares when he discovers the reason for the noise.

A small truck has parked on his lawn a couple of meters away from where the pool is, doors flung wide open with speakers pumping the volume to the fullest extent.

A MINOR ADDICT

About a hundred or more teenagers dance and shake their bodies to the thunderous beat. A lot of alcoholic beverages have been consumed in the short time that Nick has gone out. Nick walks straight to the young boy standing at the truck's door, and indicates to him to turn the volume down.

"You weren't invited as far as I can recall, for the plain reason that I don't know you, nor any of these other faces who are here now. I'll give you two minutes to take whomever you brought with you, and get the hell off my property! You're not welcome here, this gathering is on invitation only, so scram before I call the cops and get your asses locked up!"

"Daddy, please don't make such a fuss over nothing!"

Shelley tries to stop everyone from leaving, but the youngsters have already started leaving, and Nick is adamant.

"Shelley, go inside. We'll talk later. Everyone still here after the next two minutes, will answer to the police. Get out, the party's over!"

Teens run around to gather their belongings, and jump on the back of the small truck for a ride home, slapping on the rooftop.

"C'mon, let's get out of here man, before he calls the cops! Crashing the party's not worth going to jail for. Let's roll!"

In less than two minutes everyone has left, Nick's threat slams home like a six. Two of Shelley's friends arrange earlier on to stay overnight, and because there is a two-bedroomed flat separate from the house, they have given their permission.

They are also now the only two left, but are like all the rest, intoxicated from the alcohol they have ingested in just a short while. Nick sends them off to bed, and realizes that it won't help talking to Shelley, as she too, is intoxicated. She won't pay attention to what Nick has to say, and will probably not even remember half of it tomorrow. Shelley goes to bed feeling very sick.

In the months following the pool-party, Nick enforces very strict rules to keep anything similar from happening again. Shelley is restricted to school and back, nothing more.

Family life improves a little, and things return to just about the way they've been before moving to the city. Nick and Constance both sigh an inward sigh of relief. At least they don't have to tread on eggshells any longer. It sure feels good!

CHAPTER THREE

January 2009.

Nick is informed that the owner has decided to move back into her home, and the Callahan's are given thirty days' notice to evacuate the premises. Fortunately, Shelley's friend at school informs her about someone looking for tenants to take over their lease.

It's one block away from the high school that Shelley at-tends, and that means no more traffic for Nick. They go and have a look, and are so impressed with the house, that they immediately make an appointment to see the Realtor who has the house listed.

Nick takes a day off work to move their furniture into the new house and, after settling in late that afternoon buys take a ways. Everybody is exhausted, and an early night does it for them. By nine o'clock the house is totally dark and quiet, the new residents bushed from the days' work.

Shelley is up to her old tricks again, and has had plenty of boyfriends since the New Year has started out. There are forever young boys coming around after school and during the week, and Nick has told Constance that he will not stand for it. Shelley's grades have already started slipping again. After a couple of warnings from Nick, the situation persists and what makes things worse, is the fact that Nick and Shelley can't see eye to eye anymore. She questions and rebels against every decision and rule there has always been in the household, making it impossible for anyone to get along with her.

To top it off, Nick doesn't like her latest boyfriend one bit, and Shelley knows this as well as her boyfriend does. His name is Luke, and he is and looks everything that Nick despises of in a guy. Long, straight, shoulder-length hair, eyes set too close together, with an unhealthy white complexion and a face that reminds Nick of 'The Grim Reaper.'

He wears oversized clothes that are too big for him, and Nick has an uneasy feeling that the youngster is doing drugs, he just can't prove it. Whenever Nick speaks to him, he can't look Nick straight in the eye, which just proves Nick's point; the guy is sneaky and has shifty eyes.

The fact that Nick finds out later that he was at school with Luke's stepfather, does not alter the situation, for him and Nick have never been friends in school. One evening during the week, Luke arrives unexpectedly. Nick decides that he's had enough. He signals for Luke to follow him outside.

"Luke, I've spoken to both you and Shelley about this on numerous occasions, but you don't seem to understand what I said. Now I'm telling you for the very last time, and you'd better listen good. I don't want you here during the week when Shelley has school. You can come and visit her on a Friday and Saturday, and that's it. If you don't like it, that's too bad. I don't feel sorry for you, and I don't care what Shelley says. She's my daughter, and she's not twenty one yet. Me knowing your stepfather, doesn't change a damn thing, you hear me? Now, I'll give you five minutes to say goodbye to Shelley, and then you stay the hell away until Friday evening at seven, understand? I don't want this conversation again. Next time I won't be so friendly."

The shock and astonishment on Luke's face is what Nick had hoped to accomplish.

"But...but mister Callahan, I thought ..."

"That's just it, you thought. Don't think; leave that to me. I'm Shelley's father, so I'll decide what's best for her and what not. You have four minutes left to say your goodbyes. Make those four minutes count; it isn't a lot of time."

Nick turns around and leaves Luke standing outside. A couple of seconds later Luke comes inside and walks to where Shelley is busy making coffee in the kitchen. Nick hears whispering, and then Shelley comes out, followed by Luke. Nick knows by the look on her face, that she's been told the bad news. Her face has gone white, and her eyes are spitting Lava.

"Daddy ..."

"That's enough, Shelley. We've spoken about this a couple of times before, and it's no longer funny. I've nothing more to say to either of you. Time's up, Luke. I'll open the gate for you."

Constance comforts Shelley when Nick comes back inside. Upon Nick's return, Shelley darts from the dining room, slamming the bedroom door behind her, crying and sniffing as if her world has just ended. Constance looks questioningly at Nick and asks "What happened out there, Nick? What did you say to Luke that upset Shelley so much?"

"Enough is enough, my girl. You know how many times before we've spoken to them about the matter of not visiting during the week, and do they listen? No, they just carry on like nothing's been said, and I'm tired of having to repeat myself over and over. Shelley should concentrate on her grades that are so bad. Instead, she wastes away her time with that no- good low-life skunk. I'm telling you Constance, she's smoking weed with him, and Lord knows what else! I feel sick just thinking about it! Her sudden mood changes, this new attitude of hers, I'm telling you she's on something else besides weed, and if I ever find out that he's supplying her with the goods she's on, so help me God, I'll slit his throat."

Constance knows that Nick is very upset about Shelley's attitude and her open disrespectful behavior towards them. It hurts them both to see their daughter slipping away. Constance and Shelley are still getting along in a way, but only just.

"It's going to be alright, Nick. I know what you're saying is true, but let's hope it's just a phase she's going through."

"Yes, let's hope so, but I very much doubt that it's the case. I have this feeling in the pit of my stomach that nothing good's going to come of this relationship between Shelley and Luke. All it takes is that one guy to destroy a girl's life completely, and to drag her down the gutters. Girls are very susceptible to what boys think of them, and will do almost anything to keep them. I don't know what the hell's wrong with this generation of youngsters. They're supposed to be the leaders of tomorrow? With eight out of every ten being dependent on some sort of drug, I can't see that happening."

"You go and take a nice, hot shower, and I'll make you some hot Cocoa. How's that sound? I knew that would grab your attention, now off you go. I'll join you in a few."

Constance glances at Nick as he walks down the corridor towards their bedroom ...

Everything goes downhill after that, with the household in a shambles. Shelley is expelled on two occasions, the first time for bunking school, and the second for being involved in a fist-fight at school with another girl.

The fight is sent as a video clip to everyone in possession of a cell phone, and within a short while Shelley is known as the Queen Bee. She is now infamous and a legend in school, and the fact that her schoolwork and grades have turned to shit, does not seem to bother her in the least.

A MINOR ADDICT

Friday, 8 May 2009.

Shelley asks her parents for permission to spend some time with Luke at his parent's house, promising to be back within her curfew. Both Nick and Constance agree, and seizing the moment, Shelley explains that Luke's friend will come to pick her up and bring her back again.

At six thirty Nick hears a car pull up outside, and looking through the window, sees that it has stopped alongside the curb in the street. Shelley hastily comes out of her bedroom and before anybody can utter a word, she whisks out the front door with a "Don't wait up for me, I have a key!", and is out and gone.

Nick turns to Constance, an expression of utter disbelief on his face when he asks "What just happened here? She didn't even greet us properly; disappeared like mist before the sun. I don't have a good feeling about this. How are we supposed to know that it was Luke's friend who picked her up? We didn't even see the guy."

Constance can see that Nick is heavily upset, and she too doesn't feel any the better. She comes up with a suggestion.

"Let's call Luke's house and make sure whether they're really watching DVD's tonight, honey. I'll speak to Luke's mother; just relax. We'll have this sorted out in no time."

Without any further ado, Constance calls Luke's mother on her cell phone. After several rings, she answers.

"Good evening; Helen speaking."

Constance quickly explains her reason for calling, and is shocked to the core when Helen replies she has no knowledge of any such plans having been made. As far as she knows, Shelley and Luke have had a fight, and are not on speaking terms with one another.

"As a matter of fact," Helen says, "Luke is shooting some pool with his father in the entertainment area right at this minute, and his friends are here as well."

Constance goes rigid with shock.

"Thank you, Helen. I apologize for bothering. Have a good evening."

Nick knows by the way that Constance looks at him, that something is wrong. He is too afraid to ask.

"Don't tell me, let me guess. Shelley's not there, is she? If they're not there, where in tarnation are they; could Helen tell you anything?"

"Nick, you've got it all wrong, honey. Luke's at home, playing pool with his father and friends. He and Shelley haven't spoken for the last couple of days, because they've had a falling out. Helen says the reason they had words, was because of some party Shelley wanted to go to, and Luke refused. One thing led to another, upon which Shelley said that she'd go alone. It looks like she followed through with her threat."

"Well, well. Why am I not surprised to hear this? Do we have any cell phone numbers of Shelley's friends that we can call? I'm sure at least one of them will know something. Clark, come here quickly. Do you have any numbers of your sister's friends we might call?"

"Yes, I have a couple of numbers, dad. Let me write them down for you quickly. Don't know whether they still exist, 'cause these kids change numbers like a Chameleon changes colors."

Nick can't help but smile at this comparison of Clark's. He finds it quite fitting.

Constance has, in the meantime, already called a few of Shelley's friends, of whom two have answered their phones. The rest are not available. Nick and Constance keep on trying the numbers until well after midnight. It's apparent that Shelley has no intention of returning home, for it's well past her curfew.

Shelley is the type who will rather stay out the entire night and take the punishment, than stay out two hours later, and receive the same. Her motto has become, "Go big, or go home." The entire weekend is spent searching for Shelley, driving around and going to her friends' houses in order to gain more information.

xxx

Sunday, 10 May 2009; Mother's Day.

After a fruitless search the whole of Saturday and Sunday morning, Nick and Constance at last find one of Shelley's friends who knows where she has been since the Friday evening. She gives them the address of another friend in Shelley's class.

Arriving at the address, they find the boy at home, and on questioning him, find out that Shelley has been visiting with his older brother at their mother's house since Saturday morning.

The boy's father instructs his son to accompany Nick and Constance to where his brother and Shelley are after hearing what Nick has to say. It's a fifteen minute drive, and upon arriving there, the boy calls his mother on her cell phone, asking her to open the security gate to enter.

Shelley and her friend are called out after Nick and Constance speak to his mother, telling her everything. She is a judge, and says they told her that Shelley's parents were aware of the fact that she was visiting her son for the weekend. When confronted, both Shelley and her friend admit lying about it, him saying "What's the big deal? It's not like we left the country."

Nick is furious, and Constance can see by the way his hands are twitching, that Nick is close to losing it. Nick nearly tears the boy's shirt to shreds when he grabs him and pulls him closer. Nick's voice is menacing when he says "Listen to me, you little rat, and this had better sink in through your thick skull. I'm only going to say this once. You can keep on with whatever it is that you're doing, but leave my daughter out of it, you hear me? If you ever set foot near my house or Shelley again, I'll make your miserable little life not worth living for! I dislike you, and you're not welcome at my house! Shelley, get in the car, we'll talk when we get home."

The boy's mother scolds him and says "You'd better have a good explanation ready when I'm done here, because we're having a serious talk when Shelley and her parents leave. Count yourself lucky, for Shelley's parents are entitled to open a case of kidnapping against you! Get inside and wait for me!

Constance has trouble getting Shelley in the car. Nervously Constance pushes Shelley forward and in an agitated voice says "Shelley, do as your father says, before there is more trouble! Nick, let's go home. There's nothing more here for us; Shelley's safe."

Shelley shrugs her shoulders nonchalantly and walks towards the car. Her demeanor is cantankerous. Arriving home, Nick calls Shelley into his study.

"It's time we had a serious talk, Shelley. What were you thinking while you were out enjoying yourself, without letting us know where you were? To begin with, you lied to us from the word go. Didn't it occur to you that we would like to know what you were doing? Your mother and I hardly slept anything at all, because we were driving around the entire weekend looking for you, not knowing whether you're lying in a ditch somewhere or been in an accident. Oh, so you think this is funny, do you? Well, from now on you'll have no more privileges. I'm taking your phone, and you're grounded for the rest of the year. You'll go to school and back, and that's it."

A wicked smile plays around the corners of Shelley's mouth as she looks at Nick.

"I'll go wherever I want when I want, and nobody will stop me."

"Shelley! How dare you speak to your father ..."

"Shut up, mom! I'm tired of your constant wining. See if I care. Do whatever makes you happy. Here's my cell phone. Burn it if you like; I'll have another by tomorrow afternoon. I don't owe anybody an explanation of where I go to or whom I go around with. I'm nearly seventeen, and you treat me like a baby! I'm sick and tired of all your rules! From now on I follow my own rules, and there's nothing you can do."

Nick shakes his head as he denies this fact.

"Just remember, Shelley; you're not eighteen yet, so you will do as your mom and I say! Is that clear? You're not too big for a spanking, young lady."

Shelley laughs and steps forward, pointing Nick with her index finger.

"You think you can pull that one off? Try laying a finger on me, daddy dearest. I'll have you locked up so fast it'll make your head spin. I did it once; I'll do it again, and this time I won't have any charges dropped!

Nick looks at Shelley as if he's seen a ghost. He can't believe his ears! Is this a nightmare he will awaken from shortly, or did he really hear Shelley threaten him like that?

Nick is so astonished that he can't utter a word, and Shelley takes this as her queue. Before Nick or Constance can say anything else,

Shelley turns on her heels and strides out of Nick's study, slamming her bedroom door behind her.

"Well, now that was an unexpected turn of events, my girl", Nick says to Constance as he raises himself from his chair. "What do you gather from what just happened here? I honestly don't know what to do next, to tell you the truth. She's bowled me out for the time being; rattled my brain a bit."

Constance comes to stand in front of Nick, facing him.

"I don't know, Nick. I'm just as taken back by Shelley's behavior and attitude as you are. It's like she's going out of her way to disappoint us, but why would she want to do such a thing? I thought I knew Shelley, but after today, I'm not sure at all. I think we'll just have to keep a closer eye on her."

xxx

During the months following this incident, things take a turn for the worst. Shelley's behavior changes radically and in December of 2009, Nick and Constance make the decision to relocate back to the country. They have had a house built there while living in the city, and it's now time to take advantage of this benefit.

It's the end of the school year for Shelley anyway, and they can enroll Shelley at the other High School to complete her senior year. It will be the perfect plan to get her away from the dilinquents with whom she's been mixed up for the past two and a half years. A month's notice is given to the Real Estate Agency whom they've been renting from.

"Nick, I don't think we could've made a better decision than the one we just did. It'll do Shelley a world of good to be taken away from her current situation she's dug herself into. Placing her back amongst her old friends, would maybe make her see how far she's gone off the path.

Maybe this is our chance to retrieve a little bit of the daughter we've lost along the way since coming here."

"I really hope and pray that you're right, my girl. A clean break from these surroundings has to have a positive influence. I'm just so glad that we'll be rid of all these low-life trash she's been associating herself with. We'll have to tell the kids that we've decided to relocate back to the country."

Clark takes the news well, although he looks a bit sad.

"We thought you'd be glad about moving back, Clark. Is anything the matter?"

"No, it's fine dad. It's just that I quite liked the fact that I could often go to the movies. I know the reason why you're doing it, and I support you all the way.

"Good to know that you're with us, son. Mom and I apologize for taking you out of your comfort zone at this point in time. We promise to make good with you again."

"Don't worry about it, dad. You know I adapt well to whatever the situation. I'll do whatever I can to make things easier for you, but if there's something specific you want me to do, just say the word."

It's settled, and for the next couple of weeks, Shelley is left to, as she so vehemently puts it, "Follow her own rules", while Nick, Constance and Clark go about packing all the clothing, crockery, and what not into boxes.

xxx

30 December 2009; 08h00 AM.

Nick backs the huge trailer that he has rented for the day, into the driveway.

During this time Shelley tries numerous times to get hold of Luke, without any success. Devastated and heart-broken, Shelley curls up on the back seat and cries herself to sleep.

Looking at his daughter, Nick feels a pang of guilt, but quickly shoves it aside. Nick is a firm believer of "You have to be cruel to be kind." This is one such time, and he won't budge.

CHAPTER FOUR

January 2010; the new residence.

The New Year begins on a good note with no further mishaps, and the Callahan's settle comfortably in their new home. However, it lasts but a short time. Six days after relocating and moving into their own home, a single call to Shelley's cellphone changes everything.

Their hopes of leaving all her misguided friends behind in the city fall apart.

The call is from Luke. He explains that his cell phone has been out of order, that being the reason why Shelley could not get hold of him. When arriving at their house and seeing that strangers have inhabited it, he'd thought that he has lost Shelley forever.

Luke further explains that he has lost all his contact numbers, but fortunately for him, ran into one of Shelley's friends. She gave Luke Shelley's number. Shelley is ecstatic. Since relocating back to the country, she's been moody and not very talkative. Her change in demeanor is miraculous.

Shelley thinks of an excuse to get to see Luke. Then it strikes her like lightning. Of course! Her aunt is getting married on the sixteenth of January, and it's barely two weeks away.

She can't go without a date, and her father will understand that. She has to speak to Nick as soon as possible. Reassuring herself, Shelley goes in search of her father, finding him working in the garage.

"Daddy, can I speak to you for a moment?"

Nick leaves what he is doing and turns to Shelley.

"Certainly, Shelley. What's on your mind? You look and sound different than earlier today; something happen?"

"Well daddy, to tell you the truth, something did happen. Luke called me. Isn't that just wonderful? Just when I thought I'd lost him forever. He wants to come and visit me!"

Nick feels a wave of rage and disappointment wash over him, and has to fight to keep control of his emotions.

"Daddy, Luke can go with me to the wedding as my date. Please? Can't he just come and visit for two weeks? That's all I ask for. I'll never ask you again, I promise. I'll go shopping with you and mom even if Luke's here. I'll do anything you and mom want, just give me these two weeks?"

Shelley's lovely brown eyes plead with Nick, and he feels his resistance crumble away.

"Alright, I'll hear what mom has to say, Shelley. We'll discuss it, and I'll have an answer for you tonight at dinner. Is that good enough?"

"Yes, thank you so much, daddy! This means the world to me. You're the greatest!"

Nick discusses the matter with Constance and addresses the circumstances regarding the outcome with Shelley while seated around the dinner table.

"Shelley, mom and I have had a talk regarding your request this afternoon. We've decided to allow it, but there are going to be conditions. So everything depends on what you have to say about the conditions. If you're going to be obstinate, or don't like the way we set up the rules, then I'm afraid it's not going to turn out good."

Shelley is for once, calm. She looks at her parents and nods her head.

"Okay daddy, let's hear it. I'm ready to take whatever you throw my way, since I'm sure that neither of you will be unreasonable."

Nick explains that they will expect of Shelley to be in bed by ten o' clock at night during the week, since she has to attend school the following day. Shelley will have to relay this message to Luke when she calls him.

If Luke has a problem regarding rules, his visit will end before it has even started. Nick also explains that Luke will be allowed to visit her for five days only including the weekend of the wedding, and that she will not be allowed to visit him at his parent's home in the city after that. That includes school holidays. Further visits from Luke in the future does not include sleeping over, even on a weekend. He is also not allowed to visit every weekend.

"It sounds fair, thank you, daddy. I'll inform Luke when he calls me. I really do appreciate it daddy; mom, and I'll do my best to keep anything from going wrong."

xxx

Wednesday, 13 January 2010.

Luke's mother, Helen, calls Constance to ask whether she can bring Luke through on the fifteenth. Constance agrees but reminds Helen that Luke is to be fetched again on Wednesday the following week. Helen agrees to have transport available to fetch Luke on the specified day.

When Shelley arrives home from school on Friday, she is pleasantly surprised and ecstatic to find that Luke has already arrived. They allocate the guest room to Luke.

That evening while having dinner, Nick once again points out the conditions to ensure that all misunderstandings are cleared out of the way.

On Tuesday morning, Nick kicks Luke out on the street as the latter refuses to earn his keep by doing a few chores around the house. He claims that he has a bad backache and is there for unable to perform any physical labor. Luke states that he prefers to lie on the bed in the guest room and take a nap.

Luke tries to linger around until Shelley arrives home from school, but Nick doesn't allow him to. When Shelley arrives home that afternoon, chaos erupts. She won't listen to reason and locks herself in her room for the rest of the day, refusing to even have dinner.

From then on in Shelley's rebellious behavior increases by the day, and she again starts disappearing over weekends without coming home from school on a Friday afternoon. Nick and Constance find out later that it's Luke and his friends who are responsible for picking Shelley up after school.

Nick places a call to Luke's stepfather, and in no uncertain terms threatens to call the police and charge Luke with kidnapping, since Shelley is not yet eighteen.

Luke's stepfather brings Shelley back home immediately, and Nick warns Luke to stay away from Shelley or face the consequences. Luke immediately ends the relationship with Shelley. Shelley spends a couple of months getting over it, sometimes crying herself to sleep. Nick's heart goes out to her, but he knows that it will benefit Shelley in the long run.

After two months everything is smooth sailing again. Shelley makes new friends at school who are a rough crowd and do as they please.

A MINOR ADDICT

Nick and Constance decide to give Shelley some more space and extend her curfew over weekends.

Although she is given more freedom, this doesn't seem to satisfy Shelley's craving for trouble. Again she starts disappearing weekends, but she is now eighteen and according to law, an adult.

Friday night/Saturday morning, 25 July 2010-12h45am.

Nick's cell phone rings just as he is about to switch off the light and slide in between the sheets. Constance is also still awake, as Shelley's where a bouts are unknown. They have tried every possible way to get hold of her, without success. Nick sees that it's an unknown number, but decides to take the call.

"Hello, Nick Callahan speaking. Whom am I speaking to?"

Nick puts the cell phone on speaker so Constance can follow the conversation.

"Mister Callahan, this is Captain Masters from the South African Police."

"What can I do for you, Captain?"

"I apologize for calling you at this time of the morning, mister Callahan. I have your daughter, Shelley, in custody. She has been arrested for theft and is being detained in our cells. Unless you come to the Police station to discuss the matter at hand, she will be incarcerated until Monday morning when she will appear in court. Will it be possible for you to come?"

Nick is caught totally off-guard and is so shocked that he has difficulty talking.

"Hello? Mister Callahan, are you there?"

"Uhm ...yes, I'm here, Captain. Which Police station is she at?"

Nick is given the address and immediately replies.

"We're about an hour and thirty minutes' drive from there. Will you at least give us enough time to get there?"

A MINOR ADDICT

Captain Masters replies "Yes mister Callahan, I'll give you two hours to get here. If you fail to show up within that time, I won't have any other choice but to book her and lock her up."

Nick thanks the Captain and hangs up his phone. Constance is already up and starts getting dressed. She is anxious to get going and is nervous.

"Come Nick, let's leave at once; our time to get there is limited. I'll wake Clark while you get dressed."

Ten minutes later they're on their way to find out what the story behind the problem really was. Halfway there, Nick tells Constance to contact the Captain and inform him that they are on their way, and will be there shortly.

Nick breaks the speed limit at times. Constance can see that Nick isn't happy with the situation, and speaks calmly to him.

"Nick, please don't go haywire when we get there. I think things might just go better if you show some discipline and control your anger. The Captain did us a favor by calling us. I don't think they usually do things that way."

"Yes, my girl, I know. What was she thinking when she did whatever? I suppose she was out drinking with her friends again. Lord knows what else might have happened! I'm telling you; I'm fed up with Shelley's ways. If she doesn't pull herself together after this, she's out of the house when she's finished her senior year in a couple of months. I won't tolerate her behavior any longer! She's disrupting the entire family. You can know for sure that this story's going to come out sooner or later, and what are we supposed to say then to both our families? I'm stunned; I don't know what to do or say. I'll do as you've asked; listen before I say anything. Here we are!"

Nick and Constance enter the Police station with Clark on their heels. Nick sees Luke and one of his friends sitting on a bench close to the counter, and feels his blood pressure rising. Before Nick can say anything, a large-framed black man calls out to Nick and comes around the counter.

"Are you mister Callahan?"

He stretches out his arm and shakes Nick's hand when the latter replies "Yes, and you must be Captain Masters?"

The officer nods his head when he says, "I am. Please follow me into that office, mister Callahan. There is someone waiting in there who would like to speak to you. I will be present during the conversation if there is no objection."

"It's alright Captain. I have no objection to you being present."

Captain Masters opens a door and enters the office, with Nick close behind him.

"And that is the story, mister Callahan. I'm sorry about the entire thing mister Callahan, but I'm sure you'll understand that I had to act. If I didn't, I might have been out of a job on Monday morning. I don't believe that your daughter could be the only culprit here, if you take into consideration how many youngsters were at the gathering, and how much alcohol and drugs were on the premises. I saw what some of the kids looked like, and it wasn't very reassuring. Of course the drugs had been disposed of by the time we arrived there, but with my years of experience one learns to sum up the scenario very quickly. You are free to take your daughter home with you mister Callahan. I wish you well, and hope that you will be successful in sorting out whatever the problem is."

Nick thanks Captain Masters and walks out of the charge office, followed by Constance and Shelley. Clark is dragging along behind them, complaining that he won't be able to go back to sleep at that time of the morning. The time is 04:15AM.

During the following couple of days Constance makes it her priority to find out what exactly happened at the party where Shelley has managed to get herself arrested.

Constance is surprised but not shocked to find out later that Luke was the culprit who had actually stolen the cell phone and exchanged it for drugs.

The drugs that were so freely available at the party was Acid. Shelley also took some. This is a huge disappointment to her parents and Clark. As Constance understands it, Acid is a very dangerous drug to take, as it often has lethal repercussions for the user.

* LSD or Acid is also known as trips, microdots, tabs or blotters. It's often named after the designs on blotter paper, like Black Star, Orange Sunshine, Ying-Yang, and so on. Other street names are: Boomers, Dots, Golden Dragon, Heavenly Blue, Hippie, Loony Toons, Lucy in the Sky with Diamonds, Pane, Purple Heart, Superman, Window Pane, Zen.

Acid is a powerful hallucinogenic drug that alters your perception of the outside world.

LSD(Acid) is one of the most potent mood-changing and hallucinogenic chemicals. It stands for Lysergic Acid Diethylamide. LSD is manufactured from ergot, a fungus that grows on rye. It dissolves in water and is odorless, colorless, and tasteless.

Acid can, and will, turn you into a gibbering, giggling wreck and make the world seem like magical. During the course of a trip, the entire universe can turn upside down. Colors become deeply intense and everyday objects take on bizarre, wonderful new forms.

A MINOR ADDICT

All senses become confused and distorted. Some users become panicky and suffer from paranoia. Usually coming in the form of small squares of paper or tiny pellets, acid can take anything from 20 minutes to 2 hours to take effect. Trips usually last around 7 to 12 hours. There's no real way of knowing how strong a tab is or how it will affect you.

<u>Hallucinogenic drugs:</u>

Hallucinogens are substances that distort one's perception of reality. While under the influence of drugs like LSD (Acid), a user has:

1. Delusions.
2. Sees images.
3. Hears sounds.
4. Feels sensations that feel like they are really happening but are not real.

Hallucinogens produce rapid, intense mood swings and the user feels several emotions simultaneously. Acid is not the only hallucinogen. There are scores of others, such as:

1. MDMA(ecstasy).
2. PCP(angel dust).
3. Cannabis.

LSD (Acid) is the yardstick against which all other hallucinogens are measured.

<u>Side effects:</u>

Expect to make a complete and utter fool of yourself after taking acid. You will quite probably:

1. Bellow loudly at the sight of a tea-cup.

2. Converse with the trees.
3. Talk complete gibberish for hours on end.
4. Annoy anyone within a ten yard radius.

1)LSD distorts the perception of reality, by interfering with the brain's ability to selectively store immediate experiences.

2)The main part of the brain, the cortex, is overwhelmed with sensory input.

3)This flooding of information that you are experiencing, storing and comparing with past experiences is believed to be the basis of the psychedelic experience.

<u>Users also experience:</u>

1)Flashbacks days or even weeks after taking acid, where it can feel like they're reliving certain elements of their trip.

2)The drug produces delusions and visual hallucinations (light, colors, and shapes are altered, and imaginary objects appear), often including images like bleeding or melting walls, or shimmering effects.

LSD (Acid) related hallucinations and changes in perception have caused users to:

1)Panic or feel they are losing their minds. 2)Some Acid users experience severe, terrifying thoughts and feelings of despair, fear of losing control, or fear of insanity and death while using it.

3)Acid-users also lose their sense of time.

<u>*Symptoms of Acid (LSD) abuse:</u>

1)Dilated pupils.

2)Salivation or dry mouth.

3)Tingling fingers or toes.

4)Weakness.

5)Mood swings.

6)Erratic behavior.

7)Anxiety.

8)Depression.

9)Disorientation or paranoia.

10)Dizziness.

11)Nausea.

12)Rapid heart rate and convulsions.

13)Sweating or chills.

14)blurred vision.

<u>Health Risks:</u>

LSD use can cause the following short term physical symptoms.

1. Dilated pupils
2. Dizziness.
3. Dry mouth.
4. Numbness.
5. Tremors.
6. Heavy perspiration.
7. Bad body odor.
8. Goose bumps.
9. Loss of appetite.

10. Muscle weakness.
11. Trembling.
12. Poor coordination.
13. Sleeplessness (Insomnia), and
14. Palpitations.

<u>Long-term Effects of Hallucinogens:</u>

Heavy and long term abuse of LSD(Acid), mushrooms or mescaline:

1)Psychological dependence.

2)Cross-tolerance (the need for increasing amounts to feel effects; including other hallucinogens).

3)Anxiety4)Increased risk of developing schizophrenia or psychotic episodes.

5)Miscarriages.

6)Birth defects.

7)Fatal liver damage (if a bad mushroom is ingested).

8)Hallucinogen Persisting Perception Disorder (HPPD)

9)Visual disturbances.

10)Depression or panic attacks long after use.

11)Schizophrenia.

12)Severe depression.

LSD (Acid) rehabilitation treatment is different from most other drugs that are addictive. The basic LSD (Acid) treatment is to care for the person and help them become calm and stress free.

A MINOR ADDICT

<u>Psychotherapy helps former users of LSD</u>:

1. Address the confusion and fear that could be associated with HPPD (hallucinogen persisting perception disorder). After experiencing a flashback, patients report feeling guilty or fearful that they have brain damage.
2. Cognitive behavioral therapy can teach the addict how to manage triggers and flashbacks.

Shelley becomes totally uncontrollable. Her grades are slipping and she is in trouble at school on a regular basis. Nick and Constance have been called in on various occasions by the school's guidance counsellor to try several programs, but they run out of options in the end.

During the trimester exams, Shelley just disappears in the middle of the week and never returns home. No matter how Nick and Constance try, they can't get hold of her. None of Shelley's friends have seen nor heard from her.

A missing person's report is filed. Exactly one week after her disappearance, Nick receives a call from the school guidance counsellor, asking him to go and see her.

On his arrival at her office, Nick is informed that Shelley has contacted the guidance counsellor, asking for help to return home. She has also missed an examination paper in one of her major subjects that morning.

"Mister Callahan, Shelley has given me the address where she has been staying for the past week. It's about an hour's drive from here. When will you be able to fetch her and bring her back? I will speak to the Department of Education concerning the exam paper she didn't write."

Nick finds himself at a loss for words. He shakes his head in denial at this request.

"You don't understand. I'm not going to fetch Shelley. She can stay where she is. She keeps on making trouble, and everybody just keeps on bailing her out. As long as that is the case, she isn't going to stop doing as she pleases. Shelley has to realize that her actions carry consequences. We love her, but detest what she's doing to herself. If she wants to come home, she can see that she gets here the same way she managed to leave!"

The guidance counsellor is somewhat surprised at Nick's reaction.

"We can't just ignore her plea for help, mister Callahan. Would you mind if I drive there to pick her up? I have to have your permission for her to travel in my car, so please think carefully about it."

Nick nods his head and replies, "It's alright. You may go and fetch her if you like. I'd like to hear what excuse she's going to come up with this time. We've heard all the excuses there are plus a couple more she invented."

Shelley returns with the guidance counsellor, but refuses to live at home. When asked where she wants to stay, she choses to stay with friends which neither Nick nor Constance like. The young people are also always in trouble and have problems with alcohol for one.

Nobody listens to Nick and Constance when they object. In the end they decide to stop trying to help Shelley, and allow her to make her own decision.

A MINOR ADDICT

Two and a half months later; November 2010.

Nick and Constance have not had any contact with Shelley for two and a half months after she has moved out to stay with her "friends" on the other side of town. The school counsellor calls at regular intervals to let them know how Shelley is doing. Not all of them who live in the house, works. Nick manages to find the owner of the property, and arranges an appointment to speak to her.

Talking to the owner, Nick and Constance are informed that she has evicted everybody who has been living in the house, because illegal substances are being used on the property. Wild parties have been going on; sometimes throughout the night during the week.

Neighbors have started complaining, and the Police have decided to raid the property. Fortunately, when the Police go to raid the property, Shelley is not there. Three of the other occupants living there are arrested and incarcerated for the illegal possession and use of narcotics.

The guidance Councelor contacts Nick and Constance the following day. They are requested to come to the school as there is a problem with Shelley. Arriving at the school, the Guidance Councelor informs Nick and Constance that Shelley was seen sniffing a white powdery substance through her nose. Constance asks to see Shelley before further decisions are made.

The school Counselor opens her office door and beckons with her hand. Shelley; or at least someone who resembles Shelley, enters the office. Constance gasps as she takes in the appearance of the young girl entering the office. The girl's hair is uncombed and disheveled. It's obvious that she hasn't washed in days. Her skin has dark blotches on it, and her clothes are dirty and wrinkled. The white socks are brown.

"Shelley? Constance sobs. What's happened to you? I hardly recognized you. Come; sit down here."

Nick informs the guidance-councilor that he has brought a drug test with to test Shelley. When Shelley hears this, she jumps up from the chair and shakes her head. Her eyes are large with fright as she looks from her parents to the guidance counsellor.

"You can't do that without a court order! I won't do it!"

Nick intervenes. He is furious.

"Now look here, missy. We can do this the easy way or the hard way. Either you co-operate, or we take a drive down to the Police station. I have some friends there in high places, so don't make this any more difficult than it already is. Mom will go to the ladies' room with you so you can pass some urine in a sample bottle to be tested. I'll wait right here. The decision's yours. Make it snappy; we don't have all day to waste!"

With Shelley in tow, both Constance and the school guidance counsellor accompany Shelley to the restroom where a sample of her urine is taken. The minutes drag by endlessly.

After five minutes Constance walks over to where they have placed the test. Looking at it her eyes become wide with shock and her face turns white. She turns to Nick, and looks in the direction of Shelley and the counsellor.

"Nick, the ... the test is positive. Four of the five lines are blue!"

Nick goes around the desk to where the drug-test lies. Looking at the container it has come in, he quickly reads the results as are indicated on the box.

"It says here that Methamphetamines are present in her urine, my girl. That would be a substance like Cat, and it must have been used quiet recently. This proves without a doubt that Shelley has been taking drugs."

Nick looks over at Shelley, who is staring at the floor.

"What do you have to say for yourself Shelley? Do you think that you have accomplished what you set out to do; have you embarrassed us and yourself enough? I'm taking you to the Police station when we leave here. I think there might be someone in the Narcotics department who would love to hear about this. They have ways of extracting information from drug users. Who supplied you with the rubbish? We've always thought of you as smart and clever, Shelley, but this just proves the opposite, doesn't it? We're disappointed in the things you choose to do. It doesn't show much character."

The school guidance counsellor comes forward and intervenes at this point.

"Mister Callahan, I don't think you should be saying things like that to her. It's going to cause more harm than good. Leave her with me for a while and go somewhere where you can cool down. You're not thinking straight at the moment."

"There's nothing the matter with my judgement, I'll have you know. Thank you for calling us, but we'll be on our way now. We will take it from here."

Taking Shelley, they leave the school. Nick drives straight to the Police station. Arriving there, they ask to see the Chief of the Narcotics department. They are shown into an office. The man sitting behind the desk frowns as he looks up, then points at chairs.

"Please sit down ,Nick. How can I help you today?"

Shelley is very quiet, and hasn't said anything since they have left the school. It's Nick who speaks first as he points towards Shelley.

"John, I don't know how to tell you this, but Shelley ..., hell, she's on drugs, man. How can we stop this from happening again, and can you get her to give up the name of her supplier?"

John Castellino shakes his head and replies "Nick, I can't tell you how many parents I see each day with exactly the same problem as you and Constance. Unfortunately, these youngsters, and he points to Shelley, don't and won't give up the names of their suppliers. They stick to them like magnets, and that is our problem. We don't have the manpower to follow each and every one who takes illegal substances. The dealers know this, and they exploit it to the fullest. When we do catch them, it's never the big fish. There's always some technicality they get away with, but we're aware of what's going on, and we will catch them, make no mistake about that!"

Nick is shocked, and doesn't know what to say at first.

"So you're saying that for the time being, there's nothing we can do? We have to sit idly by and watch our children being manipulated and destroyed by some money-hungry drug lords who have no conscience about the lives they're destroying in the process? Isn't there some kind of punishment for the users of these substances?"

The Superintendent shakes his head.

"I'm afraid there's nothing we can do to the user's mister Callahan, unless we catch them when they're in possession of an illegal substance. Then we can arrest and incarcerate them. Other than that, the Law doesn't give us much leverage. I would suggest you don't let your daughter out of your sight. Keep a short leash on her for as long as you're able."

CHAPTER FIVE

Two weeks after the incident at school, Shelley mentions that she would like to introduce a friend to Nick and Constance. They agree and tell Shelley to invite him over for a barbeque, but question Shelley about her new friend.

"Shelley, is he still in school or does he work? If he works, what type of work does he do, and where does he come from? I'd like to know a little about him before you have him over."

"He's a senior representative with a large paint company daddy, and makes a decent living. He drives a company car and lives with his uncle and aunt not far from us, although his parents live in another State about four hour's drive from here. You and mom will like him when you meet him. He's a little older than I am and ..., wait for it. You'll love this part. He's very quiet; just like you, daddy."

Constance smiles at Nick. She knows that Nick doesn't like loudmouth youngsters, especially boys. Nick is of the opinion that the louder the mouth, the less brains there is. She also knows that it will score major points with Nick if Shelley's friend is neat in appearance and has a quiet personality.

"Well, that doesn't sound too bad. What did you say his age was?"

"I didn't say daddy, but he's twenty three."

"Hmm. Tell him to come on over Saturday afternoon at about four o' clock, and he doesn't have to bring his own meat."

Shelley smiles for the first time in months, and looks almost like her old self again.

Saturday, 14 October 2010.

Nick and Constance invite some friends over for the barbeque. Shelley's friend arrives twenty minutes before the time. Nick is busy getting the fire going when he arrives. Nick gives him a once over when he gets out of his car and walks to where Nick is standing beside the fire. Shelley comes out and does the introductions between her guest and parents.

"Stewart, this is my dad and my mom. Dad, mom, this is Stewart."

The young man holds out his hand.

"I'm very pleased to meet you both, mister and missus Callahan. You have a very beautiful daughter, if you don't mind my saying so."

Constance glances sideways at Nick, and knows immediately that Stewart has scored high on the scoreboard. Aside from being immaculately dressed, he is also well behaved. His hair is short and neat. Stewart is of medium height and build.

He has a sallow complexion and black hair with green eyes. When he smiles, his teeth are perfect. He has also made an impression on Constance, and she has to agree that for once Shelley has made a good decision.

Nick and Constance's friends arrive, and Constance laughs when her friend can't stop gaping at Stewart.

"Stop staring, Louise; he's much younger than you! Besides, he doesn't look like the type to go for older women, so stop drooling."

Louise comes out of her state of stupor.

"He's so cute! Where did Shelley meet him? She'd better hold onto him because I'm sure there are a lot of girls who would love to have him."

Constance shakes her head at her friend.

"You're impossible, Louise. I do agree with you though; he is handsome. Shelley really picked a good one this time around. Let's hope it lasts, because you know what the youngsters are like. Here today, gone tomorrow!"

xxx

The barbeque goes well. There's a relaxed atmosphere with everybody making light and friendly conversation. Stewart has two beers to drink before calling it quits. The Callahan's friends leave early, and Constance invites Stewart to stay for a cup of coffee.

"Thank you; that would be nice, missus Callahan."

While waiting for the water to boil, they all sit down at the dining room table. Nick hasn't had a chance to actually speak to Stewart, and takes the opportunity to do so now.

"So, Stewart, I believe you're a senior employee with a large paint company. How long have you been there? It must be quite exciting to know all the different types of products and what one can use each one for."

Stewart nods his head.

"Yes sir, it's quite interesting. I have a very large area to cover and I travel long distances about three times a week. Fortunately, the company covers my expences. When a new range of paints are introduced to the market, I have to attend a course and market them to all the retailers who sell our products. If things go as planned, I'll be getting promotion to management within the next couple of months, which will put me in an area manager's position."

Nick is very impressed with this.

"You've worked your way up the ladder in a very short time. I'm impressed; that takes some doing."

Stewart frowns as he looks at Nick across the table.

"Well, I've been with the company for eleven years, sir. I started with them right after I finished school."

There is a shocked silence for a while. Nick and Constance look at each other and back at Stewart, who has a puzzled expression on his face. Shelley stares at the table's glass top.

"Shelley?" It's Nick. "You told us Stewart was twenty three, but it doesn't quite work out if he's been working for eleven years, does it? That means you have to be around twenty eight or nine, right Stewart?"

Stewart immediately corroborates this.

"You're right, mister Callahan. I'm twenty nine, and I would understand completely if you had second thoughts about me seeing Shelley. I'd like to put your mind at ease though; I've never been married or engaged before. Shelley is the first girl in a very long time that I've been serious about."

There is a long silence while Nick observes the young man facing him. His mind is in turmoil, because he really likes Stewart. Nick can see that he has had a good upbringing and has integrity. Nick speaks after a couple of minutes.

"Look Stewart, personally myself and my wife like what we see in you. Don't you feel that an age gap of eleven years is a bit big? If you and

Shelley feel that you'd be able to handle it, then it's fine. I don't have a problem with it."

Shelley has been quiet until now, and speaks up calmly.

"Dad, mom, it'll be fine. Really, it will. Stewart isn't the type to take advantage of me. He's kind and he treats me with respect. That's all I want in a guy right now."

Constance also speaks her mind.

"It's okay, Shelley. Dad and I aren't going to stop you or Stewart from seeing each other. You're eighteen and an adult, and old enough to make your own decisions about what you want. We trust that Stewart will also help you make the right choices. Right, Stewart?"

"Mister and missus Callahan, I'll do everything in my power not to disappoint you or Shelley. As a matter of fact, I'd like to ask your permission to take Shelley with me next weekend. I want to introduce her to my parents. We'll be leaving Friday afternoon, and be back early Sunday afternoon. There are enough rooms, so Shelley will be sleeping in her own bedroom. I'll give you my cell number, as well as the numbers of both of my parents, and I promise to drive carefully."

Shelley looks pleadingly from Nick to Constance.

"Please; pretty please? I'll call you the moment we arrive at Stewart's parents' house. Promise!"

Nick nods his head.

"It's alright, Shelley. You may go with Stewart for the weekend, seeing that it's the last weekend you have free before your final exams."

Stewart's smile shows that he is genuinely pleased. He gets up and shakes Nick's hand.

"Thank you both, mister and missus Callahan. I really appreciate it. My parents are going to love Shelley! They actually asked me whether you would allow her to go with me next weekend, as they'd very much like to meet her."

xxx

Friday, 20 October 2010.

Shelley doesn't put a foot wrong the entire week preceding the weekend. Stewart picks her up as promised at exactly three o' clock the Friday afternoon. Shelley is packed and ready to hit the road.

They depart immediately after Stewart loads Shelley's bags in the car. Upon their arrival at Stewart's parent's house, Shelley calls Nick and Constance as she has promised them.

They can hear the joyful bantering in the background as Shelley speaks to them on the phone, and know that she will enjoy her weekend. Shelley laughs.

"Dad, mom, I have to go. We're just about to have dinner. I'll see you on Sunday afternoon."

xxx

The weekend is one of the greatest in Shelley's life, according to her. Stewart's mother and two sisters took Shelley out to shop on the Saturday morning after breakfast. Shelley can't find enough words to describe her weekend.

Nick and Constance listen in astonishment to the stories Shelley has to tell, while Stewart smiles and shakes his head. The sun has already set when Stewart gets up and excuses himself.

"Mister and missus Callahan, I'd like to thank you for letting Shelley go with me this weekend. My family really like her, and enjoyed her infectious and bubbly personality. Shelley and my sisters had a royal time shopping with my mother! I'll be on my way now, but I hope to see you again soon."

Nick and Stewart shake hands, and Constance hugs him.

"We're glad that you both enjoyed your weekend, and that your family likes her. It's sure to mean a great deal to Shelley."

Nick and Constance say goodbye and go inside the house, giving Shelley and Stewart some time alone. Shelley comes in after about ten minutes; her features alight with joy. She looks from Nick to Constance.

"You both seem to have taken a liking in Stewart. I'm glad. He really is super, and a real gentleman. If you ever meet his parents, you'll know why. Stewart's father and mother are like two lovebirds, but they still give each other space, and everybody in the family treat each other with the utmost respect. It's uncanny but nice!"

Clark, who has been listening to their conversation, nods his head in agreement.

"Yes, Stewart is a nice guy. I think he's the best boyfriend you've ever had, Shell, or brought home! If you let him slip through your fingers, you'll be crazy. Guys like him are hard to come by. How old are his sisters?"

Everybody laughs at this question of Clark's, and teases him about it for a while. At the end of November 2010, Stewart relocates to another town. He rents a house, and after giving her the go- ahead, Shelley furnishes the entire house to her liking.

Shelley doesn't see as much of Stewart as she would like to since he has moved. Stewart makes an effort to see her at least three times a week, even if it means only taking her out for coffee.

Shelley completes her final exams, and just when everything seems to fall in place, there is a setback. The Callahan's have planned on going to the South coast, as they do each year in December. Shelley starts acting up two weeks after completing her grade twelve exams, and packs some of her clothing when announcing that she is going to visit a friend for a while. On the day before they are to leave for their vacation, Nick calls Shelley to find out what time she will be home.

"Hallo Shelley, dad here. What time will you be home tonight? Remember, we're leaving early tomorrow morning, so we're not going to bed late. What was that? You're not ..."

"Daddy, I'm not going on vacation with you this year. It's going to be boring. We always go to the same place. I'm just not up to it; sorry."

"Shelley, what are you going to do? Where do you plan on staying until we return? I'm not leaving you the keys to the house, if that's what you want!"

"It's fine dad. Don't worry, I've always managed in the past."

"If you do decide to go with, you still have time until tomorrow morning to let us know, okay?"

"I'm not going with, dad. Don't you understand what I've just told you? Just stop it! Have a good vacation; I'll see you when you get back. Bye for now."

Before Nick has a chance to react to her last remark, Shelley goes offline. Constance, who has been following the conversation, looks at Nick with a puzzled expression in her eyes.

"What's the matter Nick? As far as I can tell by your conversation, Shelley's refusing to go on vacation with us. What's her excuse this time to wiggle herself out of our company?"

Nick is not sure himself, and shrugs his shoulders.

"I don't exactly know, my girl. Do we ever know why Shelley does what she does? Anyway, I think I'll call Stewart and hear whether he can save the day. Maybe he'll be able to talk some sense into Shelley."

Constance nods her head at this suggestion of Nick's.

"Yes, I think that's a very good idea you have there, my love."

Nick dials Steven's number. He answers almost immediately.

"Hi Steven, how are you doing? As you know, we're leaving for vacation tomorrow morning. Shelley has a problem, but we don't exactly know what it is. According to her, it's going to be boring. Do you perhaps have any idea why Shelley is acting this way? We were wondering whether you could be of any assistance."

"Hello, uncle Nick. I'll help in any way if I possibly can."

"Shelley hasn't been home for almost a week, and I've just spoken to her on the phone. She refuses to go on vacation with us. However, I think there's more to it than that. She seems a little off the rails, if you know what I mean."

There is an awkward silence at the other end of the line.

"Hello? Steven, are you there?"

"I'm here Uncle Nick. I suspected as much when you said there was a problem and that it was Shelley. I don't know what's wrong with her. She doesn't want to stop hanging out with those friends of her. I've pleaded with her, but she's very obstinate about it. What do you suggest we do, uncle Nick?"

"Well, I was thinking it might be a good idea if you took her to your house until we return. She wouldn't object going with you, of that I'm certain. We'd also feel much better knowing she's with you than with any of her other so-called friends."

"I'll leave a little earlier than usual and fetch her from wherever she is, uncle Nick. Don't worry, I'll sort it out and give you a call once I've picked her up."

Nick sighs with relief and gives Constance a thumbs' up.

"Thank you Steven. Your help means a lot to us. We're sorry for burdening you with this."

"No need to apologize, uncle Nick. You both know how much I care for Shelley, so it's no burden. Enjoy your vacation. Say hi to aunt Constance."

Nick says goodbye and hangs up. He smiles as he reassures Constance.

"Steven says he'll go and pick her up in a while and take her to his place. Looks like Shelley will be okay after all. I feel better knowing Steven will be looking after her."

Constance also agrees to this.

"Yes, so do I Nick. At least she'll be with someone we both trust and like."

A MINOR ADDICT

13 December 2010; 04h15A.M.

Nick turns onto the highway, and joins the masses of other cars speeding towards the first tollgate. Constance is awake to keep him company, and soft music plays in the background.

Clark has gone back to sleep. Nick and Constance have decided to ask Nick's mother along. She will be going with them for a couple of days and then visit Nick's brother at the North coast for a few days.

Quickly dawn creeps up on them, and when they reach the tollgate twenty minutes later, the sky is grey, and orange fingers stretch out to announce the beginning of a new day. Nick stops at regular intervals, giving everybody enough time to stretch their legs and go to the bathroom.

They also sit down at an Ultra-City garage for breakfast, and again for lunch. By then they have already reached the coast, and only have a couple of kilometers to travel to their destination, when Nick's cell phone rings. He sees that it's Shelley, and hands it to Constance to answer.

"Hi honey, how are you?"

Nick indicates to Constance to put the phone on speaker. Shelley has a clear voice when she speaks "Hi, mom! Where about are you guys now?"

"Oh, we're about thirty kilometers or so from our destination honey. We're travelling along the shoreline. It's beautiful, and the sea is quite calm and blue. We wish you were here."

There is momentary silence before a sob sounds softly from the other side.

"Daddy, mom; I'm so sorry that I acted the way I did yesterday. I wish I could be there with you. I miss you all so much!"

"Honey, I could buy you a bus ticket to join us. Would you like that?"

"Yes, I would daddy; very much. When can you do that? Once you've done that, just let me know where and when I should board the bus."

Constance is very happy about the turn of events, and smiles broadly.

"Daddy will book the ticket as soon as we reach our destination. I'll let him call you immediately afterwards, okay? By tomorrow this time you should be with us."

"Thank you so much, you guys. I can't wait to get there!"

After reassuring Shelley that Nick will book her ticket, they hang up and continue on towards their destination. Nick can see, and he knows, that Constance is happier now than she has been since they left their house that morning. She is smiling, and her eyes have a sparkle to them. Nick points at the sign with his index finger.

"The turn-off's just in front! We should be there in about another ten minutes."

Nick's first stop is the Mall. Him and Constance go into the shopping center and queue in line at the Money-market counter. When it's their turn, Nick enquires about the various bus timetables. The booking clerk disappoints both Nick and Constance with the news he has for them.

"I regret to inform you that all the buses are fully booked for the next week. Unless there's a cancellation, which I strongly doubt, you'll have to look at a booking for next Saturday. The bus will then stop here on Sunday morning at ten o' clock. That's the best I can do for you folks."

Nick feels his heart skip a beat. He looks at Constance, and sees that she feels the same way. Shelley won't be able to join them before their vacation is up!

"We tried, my girl. There's nothing more we can do. Let's call Shelley and tell her."

Shelley is devastated about the bad turn of events, but under-stands that nothing can be done about it. They talk for a couple of minutes more, with Constance promising to call Shelley regularly during the week.

Arriving at the beachfront apartment where they will spend their vacation, Nick and Clark carry their suitcases inside, where Constance immediately starts unpacking. Everything is neat and tidy.

Nick checks to see whether all the electrical appliances are in working order, and satisfied that everything is alright, goes outside onto the balcony.

Clark joins him, and together they watch a cargo ship with the binoculars passing on the horizon. Constance calls for Nick, and hands him a list of goods that she wants him to purchase.

"Alright, Clark and I will drive down to the shopping complex and get what you want. Is there anything else that you might have forgotten to add to the list, my girl? I'm going to get us some meat from the butchery as well."

Nick walks to where his mother is standing on the balcony, staring out to sea.

"Mom, can I get you something from the shop? Clark and I are going to the shopping complex to get a few things."

Nick's mother looks up at him and smiles.

"No, thank you, son. It's quite alright; I don't need anything right now."

Before they know it, time has come for them to take Nick's mother to the North coast, where Nick's brother will meet them. On their way there, Nick suggests that they all meet at their cousin's house. Nick calls his brother and arranges for him to pick up their mother there.

The rest of their vacation flies by in the wink of an eye, and before they know it, it's time to meet Nick's mom and brother again. They pick Nick's mother up at nine o' clock the morning, and by four thirty the afternoon they are back in their hometown.

Dropping his mother off at her home, Nick and Constance head for their own home. Constance called Shelley and Steven an hour previously, and twenty minutes after arriving home, Steven's car pulls up outside on the curb. Constance goes outside and uses the remote to let them in.

Shelley runs towards Constance who catches her in a tight hug. Steven is invited to join them for dinner, and the discussion around the dinner table hovers around her time with Steven and the family's vacation at the South Coast. Clark utters a few words.

"I have to tell you sis, you missed out on a super awesome vacation! We ate out a bunch of times, and I ate as much meat as you could imagine. We went to visit dad's cousin as well. I have to admit though; it's good to be home!"

Everybody starts laughing at Clark as he continues eating, oblivious of how funny he's said it. Clark looks up from his plate and grins back at them.

"Why are you all laughing; did I say something funny?"

Shelley clutches at her belly as she laughs and says "Oh, Clark, you're so totally hilarious; I think I'm going to wet my pants! I missed your nerdy cracks."

Clark just shakes his head and mumbles something incoherent under his breath ...

"Talk about a loony. I think she's crazy."

Laughter carries on for quite some time. Lying in bed later on, Nick and Constance both agree that it has been one of the most memorable days in a very long time.

CHAPTER SIX

Shelley has been staying with a friend for the past two months to find a job. She targets specific companies, and manages to land a job at a very reputable Law firm as a Personal Assistant to one of the company's senior partners.

xxx

Thursday, 28 April 2011.

Shelley calls Nick just after dinner, telling him that she has also managed to find a room in a commune not too far from where she works. The only problem is that she doesn't have the finances to move in. Shelley asks Nick whether he would be willing to put up the deposit as well as one month's rent in advance.

"Please daddy, otherwise I can't move in. It's not far from my offices, and one of the firm's senior partners lives close to the commune. He said I could travel to work and back with him at no charge. I'll repay every cent, I promise."

"Shelley, you know I won't take your money. It's alright; we'll be there tomorrow morning and get everything organized. You can call the owner of the commune and get his banking details for me. Tell him that I'll be doing a direct deposit. Just let me know what the correct amount is. Where can we pick you up when we get there?"

"You can pick me up at my friend's apartment daddy. I think you know where she lives; the apartments just around the corner from my old high school."

"Is it the apartment block where mom and I took you to the first time?"

"Yes, that's it daddy. Call me when you get here and I'll come down. I'll take you and mom to go and have a look at the place where I'm going to be living, okay?"

It has been three months since Shelley started her new job. Trouble starts just before the end of her third month. They haven't seen, nor heard from her in quite a while. Nick decides to call the law firm where she works and asks to speak to Shelley.

He can then at least ask her whether there are problems and why they haven't heard from her. The receptionist who answers the telephone, asks Nick whether she can put him on hold for a minute. After a couple of seconds, Nick is reconnected with a man.

"Good morning, mister Callahan. I'm David Parker, senior partner at the law firm and Shelley's employer. The receptionist informed me of your call, and I asked her to connect me with you. There's something I'd like to discuss with you, so I'm quite glad that you called in. I would have been more at ease if it was possible to speak to you face to face, but I realize that you live quite far, so I'll just come straight to the point. We've been encountering problems with Shelley for quite some time; a few weeks to be precise. I've called her in and spoken to her on two previous occasions, and she's promised me that she would pull her weight. There hasn't been any improvement though, and I don't know what the problem is. In the beginning she was a real go-getter, but it seems that something has happened to steer her off course. I'm sorry, mister Callahan, but we're going to have to let her go."

Nick doesn't know what to say.

"I apologize on behalf of Shelley for her indecent behavior at work, mister Parker. We have not heard from Shelley in a while ourselves, and can't get hold of her. That's why I decided to call the office and find out what the problem is. Now I know why she hasn't been in contact with us. Is she at work at the moment?"

"No, Shelley hasn't been in for a couple of days now. She will still be employed up to the end of this month, but I've given her the rest of the time off to look for other employment. I've already told her that she won't be staying on with us. As far as I know, she's also no longer residing at the commune where she used to. That must be why she's had problems getting to work."

"Thank you for telling me this. My wife and I will find a way to sort this out as soon as possible, if we can find her. I'll be in contact."

Nick hangs up and calls for Constance to join him. Constance joins him in the dining room and looks questioningly at Nick. She can see that Nick isn't feeling good; his face is chalk-white.

"What's the matter darling? You look like you've seen a ghost."

"My girl, I have very bad news. Come and sit down; let's talk. I just got off the phone with Shelley's boss. He informed me that they've sacked Shelley because she doesn't show up for work, and and she is consistently late. Apparently she also doesn't live at the commune anymore. What the hell's going on here? Just when things started looking good, she goes and does something like this! It's as if she doesn't want things to work out in her favor."

Nick is worked up good. He is over the initial shock. Constance bites her bottom lip and clenches her fists, not looking at Nick. The next question brings Constance back to the present.

"What's up, my girl? It looks like you have something on your mind."

Constance nods her head, her shoulders hunched forward. Her voice is a mere whisper, and Nick has to lean forward to hear what she is saying. "Nick, you remember when you let me visit her for a week about a month after she'd moved into the commune? I had a reason why I came back earlier, b ... but I didn't think that it would spiral out of control like this, or so soon. I wanted to tell you, but I knew how you'd react. That one friend of Luke's, well, he ... he came to visit Shelley while I was there. They thought that I was asleep, but I wasn't. He took out a small plastic bag half-filled with a white powdery substance. At first I didn't know what it was, then I heard both of them snorting. When I sat upright on the bed, they were both so high that they just lay there. They'd used a straw to snort up the white powder; I saw it lying next to the plastic on a piece of broken mirror! Shelley's nostrils were white from the powder. It, it was awful!"

"But ... but you never ..."

"I know, and I'm so sorry. Shelley promised me when I confronted her the next morning that she would never do it again. Two days later, that boy came to visit her again. I told him to scram, but both he and Shelley laughed at me. They got high again. When I asked Shelley what it was, she said "Ah, it's only a little CAT, mom. Don't be like that; all you ever want to do is spoil my fun!"

*The consistence of Cat:

Cat is a white or off-white powdery substance and a Methcathinone, which is very potent. It is also known as:

1. Stroof.
2. Katestroof.
3. Jeff.
4. Bathtub Speed.
5. Wannabe-Speed.
6. Kitty.
7. Meth's cat.
8. Meth's Kitten.
9. Marzipan.

Cat or Kat refers to two types of drugs.

Although they're similar, one is the leaf from the shrub Catha edulis, which contains Cathinone.

The other is a synthetic powder which contains Methcathinone and is much more potent. The people of Eastern and Central Africa, as well as parts of the Arabian Peninsula have been chewing the leaves of this shrub for centuries.

Cathinone is a natural amphetamine and an ephedrine-like substance. Methcathinone is much more potent. Both are psychoactive stimulants and part of the amphetamine family. Amphetamines trigger the release of dopamine molecules from their storage vesicles in the brain.

This causes them to flow out to the next neuron in massive quantities. They also block the re-uptake of dopamine, but this is not the principle mechanism of its effects. Dopamine is the neuro-transmitter that regulates motor behavior.

The effects usually last from four to six hours. Cat users, like users of crystal and other stimulants, often stay on "runs" for days at a time, then sleep for a day or more and start another binge.

The physical effects of Methcathinone hydrochloride:

1. Increases spontaneous rodent locomotor activity.
2. Potentiates the release of dopamine from dopaminergic nerve terminals in the brain, which causes appetite suppression.
3. Users forget to consume fluids, which leads to dehydration. This commonly causes Hypertension(High blood pressure) and Tachycardia(elevated heart rate).

This includes feelings of:

1. Euphoria.
2. Increased alertness.

3. Dilated pupils.
4. Increased heart rate.
5. Rapid breathing.
6. Inability to stop talking.
7. Increased and/decreased sexual function and desire.

Loss of cognitive ability relating to the distinction of relative importance of matters(one might spend days thinking that he/she is being productive but later realize that the activity/product was never really necessary).

Chronic high dosage results in:

1. Acute mental confusion ranging from mild paranoia to psychosis.
2. Over dosage on this drug results in what is called "amphetamine psychosis", and is a recognized psychiatric condition.

Over stimulated and deprived of sleep, the user panics and becomes violent, manifesting magnified physical strength. It feels like bugs crawling under the skin, and suffering from delusions and other paranoia can also result.

Side effects after taking the drug:

1. Enlarged pupils.
2. Heart rate increases.
3. Blood pressure increases.
4. Temperature increases.
5. Teeth grinding is common.
6. Jaw clenching is common.

Withdrawal symptoms include:

1. Lethargy.
2. Depression.
3. Nightmares.
4. Tremors.

Nick is speechless for a couple of minutes, his mind racing. His voice sounds tired when he talks.

"How did this happen, my girl? Is it something we did? I can't think where we went wrong. Both Clark and Shelley had the exact same upbringing, and Clark hasn't caused us one day of grief or stress!"

Constance takes a seat next to Nick on the sofa and holds his hand.

"I know, darling, and I'm just as upset as you are. What happened has been eating me up inside! After what you've just told me, Shelley must have got herself in so deep that she doesn't know how to get out. She is very gullible, Nick. What are we going to do? We can't just leave her; please!"

Nick sighs deeply, shaking his head.

"I don't know what we're going to do, but I do know that we have to find Shelley. When we find her, we'll know what our next step will be."

Clark is informed of the developments in Shelley's situation and decides to stay home while his parents go out to look for Shelley. The following morning Nick and Constance set out for the city, and an hour later Nick turns his car off the highway.

He heads straight for the commune where Shelley has been residing for the past three months. Fortunately, one of the men living there works nightshift, and his car is standing in the driveway. Nick raps on the front door. After a couple of minutes, the door opens to reveal a young man in his early twenties.

"Morning. Sorry for disturbing you this early, but I need to ask you some questions concerning Shelley."

The young man squints his eyes when he looks at Nick and then at Constance.

"You're Shelley's parents, right? Come on in."

"Yes, but we're not here on a social call. We need to know where she is, and I'm hoping you might be able to tell us. It really is important that we find her as soon as possible."

The youth nods his head.

"Well, I'll try and answer what I know, and that's not much. Ask away."

Before Nick can speak, Constance corners the young man.

"You were here that week when I visited Shelley. Remember?"

The young man nods his head.

"Yes, I remember. As far as I can recall, you and your daughter had a differences of opinion. You left very early on the Friday morning."

"There was a guy who came to visit Shelley twice during that week. Do you recall?"

The young man ponders this for a moment, then nods his head.

"Yes, I remember him. A real scruffy looking guy. I wondered what Shelley's relationship to him was. He was here a couple of times after you left, but then he stopped coming around. Another guy started visiting Shelley; tall, skinny. Then Shelley started sleeping here less often. I haven't seen her in a couple of days."

Nick shakes his head to get rid of the cobwebs. He can't believe what he is hearing.

"Tell me, where can I get hold of the owner of this property? I'd like to speak to him."

"I can give you his cell number; just let me get my cell phone quickly."

Nick nods his head in agreement.

"Go ahead. We're not going anywhere in a hurry."

The young man returns with his cell phone, and within seconds he retrievs the owner's number from it. Nick thanks him and returns with Constance to the car, where he dials the number the young man has given him.

Seconds later Nick is connected to the commune's owner. After Nick introduces himself, the owner tells him in no uncertain terms and without mincing words that he is not returning the deposit, as Shelley has moved out without giving notice.

He also informs Nick that he has a forwarding address for Shelley. Nick thanks him, and upon Nick's request, the owner sends Shelley's new address to his cell phone via short message service.

xxx

Nick knows exactly where the suburb is and drives straight there. They find the address without any problem. The surprise on Shelley's face when she sees her parents is worth everything they have gone through the previous couple of days.

Neither Nick nor Constance are happy with the circumstances, and gives Shelley a piece of their mind. Shelley can't come up with an excuse why she has moved out of the commune to her present address when she did have a job.

Nick makes it clear that he expects her to repay the deposit he has lost due to her negligence. Constance takes Shelley one side and questions her about the young man whose house she has moved into. Both Nick and Constance are against it.

"Mom, I don't need either of you two to give me permission for what I want to do. I'm nineteen and not a baby anymore, so quit treating me like one!"

Nick is furious with Shelley for her attitude toward them. In a stern voice Nick repremand's Shelley when he says "Shelley, don't speak to your mother in that tone of voice. Treat her with the respect that she deserves to be treated with! All we want is the best for you, we don't want to ruin your life or dictate what you're allowed to do and what not. Give us the benefit of the doubt here. We are your parents, not strangers!" "Dad, we don't live here alone! His mom and sister live here as well. It's not like we're planning on getting hitched or anything, we just like each other's company. If you don't like it, well ..."

Constance intervenes, as she can see that Nick is close to losing his temper.

"Shelley, we raised you to have high morals and standards. Do you think you're living up to them?"

"Mom, this has nothing to do with morals. I am making the decisions here, not you or dad. If I'm making the wrong choices, I want it to be on my terms. Please talk to dad. I can see he's in no mood to be reasonable. Just let me at least introduce you to the people who live here."

Constance looks at Shelley and has a feeling of disengagement from her. She turns around and walks to where Nick is standing at the gate. She takes him by his hand.

"Sweetheart, let's meet this young man. At least we now know where Shelley lives, and with whom. It's better than not knowing anything at all. This way we can keep in contact with her."

Nick shakes his head ever so slightly.

"I don't like the looks of him, my girl. He's a charmer. I had a good look at him while you were talking to Shelley. He's going to use her and then just walk away, like nothing's happened. I've seen his type operate, but I'll do it to please you, and for no other reason. Let's get it over with."

Shelley leads the way into the house and calls out to the inhabitants.

"Hey everyone, come and meet my folks!"

They exchange greetings, with Nick staring long and hard at the new "friend." His name is Marcus, and he is tall and rather skinny with a baby face, blue eyes and perfectly straight teeth. Nick decides not to beat about the bush and get straight to the point. He addresses both Marcus and his mother.

"We as Shelley's parents don't condone Shelley living with you, Marcus. I want you to know that. What the two of you are doing shows only disrespect for us as Shelley's parents, as well as your mother."

Nick doesn't sit down after he enters the house, and walks towards the door, pausing to wait for Constance. Shelley's new boyfriend can see that Nick doesn't like him. In return he shows Nick mutual disrespect with his attitude. He looks Nick up and down, shakes his head and enters a bedroom, where he shuts the door behind him.

There is no news from Shelley during the following three and a half months. Only sometimes does Constance get through on her cell phone; if she is lucky enough. Shelley never speaks long. It's as if she is trying to keep her parents at a distance. Not once over the entire period does she pay them a visit. Even Clark finds this strange behavior of Shelley a little unnerving.

Nick and Constance decide to go to the West coast for their vacation in December 2011. They will leave on the 10th of December 2011 and return on the 2nd January 2012.

A couple of days' later Constance receives a call from Shelley, and tells her about their upcoming vacation. Shelley becomes quiet at the other end of the line. Her next words rather surprise Constance.

"Mom, would you ask dad to come and fetch me, please? I'd like to go on vacation with you guys, if it's alright. I know I haven't exactly been "the good daughter" these past couple of months, but I really do miss all of you."

"Well Shelley, I don't think dad would mind. He's going to do a site visit at one of his sites on Friday. I could ask him to pick you up when he's done with his work."

"Thank you, yes. That would be fine. I'll be waiting for dad to come and pick me up Friday afternoon then. I can't wait to see you guys again!"

Constance and Shelley speak for a while longer before hanging up. It looks like the year will end on a good note ...

xxx

10 December 2011, 05:45AM.

Four vehicles travel in a convoy, on their way to a well-deserved vacation. They are well on their way, and have already made their first stop, as the women have to use a bathroom.

Shelley is in the car with Nick and Constance, with Clark catching up on his sleep. The convoy reaches its destination at 6:30PM, having made more stops than anticipated.

Their longest stop is at a natural waterhole in the mountains, where all the children jump off the side of a cliff into the cold mountain spring water.

The water is ice cold, and after the first try, everybody's heroic enthusiasm disappears. Nick and Clark fill water bottles with the cold spring water, as they have about another two and a half hour's drive before reaching their destination.

Nick's youngest brother has already been camping with his caravan for a week prior to their arrival. He starts a barbeque, and food is on the table when they arrive at the campsite. It's been a long day with a lot of miles covered, and after dinner everybody parts ways to their own holiday homes.

The vacation is an awesome experience, as it's the first time that Nick and his family have ever gone to, or seen, the West coast. It's beautiful, and Nick and Constance visit all the small little towns with their private beaches along the shoreline.

They eat the most fantastically prepared Calamari on the docks, and return a couple of days later to let Clark and Shelley have a taste. They agree that it's the best they have ever had.

It's good to see Shelley enjoy herself and start rekindling with the family. She is nearly the Shelley they have all forgotten. It turns out to be the calm before the big storm.

A MINOR ADDICT

24 December 2011.

From out of nowhere, Shelley announces that she will be spending the rest of their vacation, including Christmas day, with Marcus and his mother. They have only just arrived at the West coast after deciding to spend some time with Marcus's uncle who lives close by. It's like dropping an A-bomb. Nick's face turns white, and for a moment he seems speechless.

"What's that, Shelley? I don't believe I heard right. You said you were going to spend the rest of our vacation with Marcus and his family, and that they're coming to fetch you tomorrow? When did this happen? I saw you texting on your phone all day yesterday and this morning; were you making plans during that time?"

"Don't be so short sighted daddy. I've spent two weeks with you! Isn't that enough?"

"Shelley, you haven't been home in more than six months, and you think that two weeks makes up for it? Where's the logic in that? We'd like to have you spend all your time with us until we return home after New Year's. That isn't asking too much!"

"Daddy, I've already given Marcus the address. I can't go back on my word at the last minute! Besides, his mother decided to come down here and look for a job. Seeing that we're here for vacation, Marcus came along to spend some time with me. Isn't that considerate of him?"

"I'd call it very inconvenient and inconsiderate, Shelley. He knew you were coming here with us. I don't like the guy, and I'm not interested in getting to know him! Do whatever you like, just don't come running to me when he pulls the rug out from under you."

Shelley rolls her eyes and pulls her shoulders up nonchalantly.

"Okay fine; I will. It suits me. I'm bored here anyway."

Their conversation takes place on the beach where Nick is standing, looking out to sea when Shelley joins him and drops the bomb. Nick turns around after their conversation and quickly walks back towards the house.

Constance is standing on the porch and smiles when she sees Nick and Shelley talking. Her feeling of euphoria doesn't last long as she sees Nick walking back towards the house. She can see by the way he is walking that something is wrong. She hastily walks to Nick when he makes for the apartment they are staying in. Preventing him from going any further, she lays her hand on his arm, saying "Nick, what's the matter? It looked like you and Shelley were having such a good time talking."

Nick shakes his head and is quiet for a few seconds, hanging his head. When he looks up, Constance sees the raw emotion lying shallow in his eyes.

"Shelley just told me that she would be spending the rest of our vacation with Marcus and his family. They'll be coming for her tomorrow. It looks as if she has just been using us as usual. I told her to do whatever she wants to. It looks like we're back to square one with Shelley. I have now had it with her."

xxx

Sunday morning; 25 December 2011.

The time is close to 10h00 A.M, and Shelley is standing outside, texting on her cell phone. Nick is on his way to the camping site's ablution block to have a shower before Christmas lunch is to be served.

Shelley walks in front of Nick and heads for the security gate. Not knowing what the reason for this is, he doesn't pay any attention to it. After taking a revitalizing shower, Nick heads back to the house and sits on the porch until the whole family arrives. It's only after lunch that Nick becomes aware of Shelley's absence.

When he questions Constance about it, she is surprised to hear that Shelley did not greet Nick when leaving.

"Honey, Shelley left with Marcus when you went to shower. Now that I recall; when I asked Shelley whether she had said goodbye to you, she didn't really answer me. Things were so hectic, and she was busy introducing him to everyone. That's really nasty of Shelley."

"Yes well, I suppose I shouldn't have expected anything less than that. As a matter-of-fact, I don't feel like staying any longer. Would you mind if we went home tomorrow?"

Constance shakes her head when she looks at Nick.

"You know it would be fine by me Nick, but what about Shelley?"

"Shelley's not worried about us in the least, my girl, so why should we feel any different? No, I'm not worried. She can get a ride back with her boyfriend. He took her away here, so he can see she gets home. Let's go and pack our suitcases; we're leaving here early tomorrow morning.

Nick and Constance call Clark and tell him of their decision. They give him the choice to stay, or go home with them. Should he decide to stay behind, he can travel with Nick's mother and sister when they return. Clark shakes his head vehemently and replies "No thanks, dad. I'd much rather go back with you and mom. No offence, but to travel in the same car with Granny for one thousand miles?"

They laugh at the suggestive implications of the question. Nick calls his mother and tells her about their decision. She isn't happy, but knows that she can't persuade Nick otherwise. Constance calls Shelley on her cell phone to inform her that she is to look for another ride back home.

The following morning at 08h00AM, Nick, Constance and Clark depart, and soon they are heading Northbound on the busy highway.

CHAPTER SEVEN

———

Their retreat is something of the past. Nick, Constance and Clark await the New Year. A few days before the return of Nick's family, there is indeed a great surprise. Constance receives a phone call on her cell. The number is unknown to her, but she answers it.

"Hello? Speak up please, the line's very bad. I'm sorry, I ... Shelley! I'll call you back, maybe the line's better then. Okay, I'll call right back." Constance pulls her shoulders up and makes a face as Nick looks inquisitively at her.

"I'm as much in the dark as you are, Nick. Hang on, let me call her back and hear what she wants. She's definitely not calling to find out how we're doing. Ah, it's ringing! Hello, Shelley. This really is a surprise! We didn't expect to hear from you so soon again. You want to speak to your father? Let me just find out whether he wants to speak to you. What was that? No honey, you never even greeted your dad when you left with Marcus on Christmas day. You were very rude! Hang on a minute; he says he'll speak to you."

Nick takes the cell phone from Constance and holds it to his ear.

"Speak to me, Shelley. What was that? Don't talk so fast! Alright, I'll try not to be nasty to you. I don't think I heard that right. You don't have a ride back home? I thought you were coming back home with what's his name... uhm; Marcus. Not? So how is he getting home? Oh, I see. He's coming back with the bus? Well, tell him to buy you a ticket as well. He doesn't have money? Isn't that convenient? Okay, okay; I'll call your uncles and Granny and find out, but don't expect miracles. I'll have mom call you back on this number in about an hour or so. Bye."

Nick sighs and sits down on the sofa. He indicates to Constance to sit down beside him. It's her turn to look at Nick questioningly.

"Well, what did she say?"

"Shelley says she doesn't have a ride back home. She and Marcus have had a fight and he's dropped her. He's getting on the bus. Shelley wants me to ask one of my brothers or my mother whether they could give her a ride back home. Let me call and find out. I told her you'd call back."

After calling both his brothers and his mother, Nick shakes his head at Constance when he puts his cell phone down.

"I'm afraid not one of them are willing to help her out. Can't say that I blame them. Apparently there was a little trouble after we left. Shelley and her boyfriend helped themselves to cigarettes and pies while the others were outside. When confronted about it, they denied that they'd done it. They were chased away. My family doesn't want anything to do with Shelley. She's on her own. I warned her about that scoundrel and his underhanded methods! I hope she's learnt a lesson!"

"What is she going to do Nick? How will she get back home?"

"I don't have the slightest idea, my girl. Don't panic; we'll sort something out. Just let me think for a while."

Constance is once again aware of how safe she feels when Nick is at the helm. She knows without doubt that he will find a solution to this obstacle.

"Call Shelley and ask to speak to her ex-boyfriend's mother, then hand me the phone."

Nick takes the cell phone from Constance and speaks briefly to Marcus's mother. After a brief conversation with her, Marcus' mother offers to pay for Shelley's bus fair home and Nick arranges with Shelley where he will pick her up. Everything is sorted out in a matter of minutes. Constance thanks Nick after speaking briefly to Shelley.

Four days later Nick and Constance pick Shelley up at a Shell garage, where the bus makes its last stop before carrying on to the depot. Shelley and Marcus are seated a few rows apart. There is no talking before she exits the bus.

Nick is inside the garage's tuck shop when the bus stops, and as he steps out of the tuck shop, the bus leaves. This suits both Shelley and Constance, as they know what Nick intends to do. He is on a warpath, and threatens to hurt Marcus if he ever crosses paths with him again.

So it happens that Shelley is once again at the mercy of her parents, and living with her parents, very much against her will. She is not happy with circumstances or the way things have worked out for her. What's more is the fact that she has to admit that Nick is right about Marcus. He's a player, but a very handsome one at that!

xxx

Shelley stays with her parents on and off for a period of two months, more often than not visiting friends in the city and staying away for long periods of time. Shelley arrives home one day in April 2012 and announces that she is relocating back to the city.

She goes for an interview at an advertising company, and lands the job as a personal assistant to the managing director. Shelley also manages to find a place to stay not far from her new work, and can travel with one of her co-workers. It's a good opportunity and the salary is good for a beginner who knows nothing about advertising.

Everything goes well for almost four months. The Callahan's often pay Shelley a visit over weekends. During this time, Marcus appears on the scene again, but Shelley keeps him at bay.

A MINOR ADDICT

One evening, while visiting at a club with friends, Marcus shows up at the club and pulls Shelley to one side, complaining about his father's unreasonable attitude towards him. Marcus's father wants him out of his house. Shelley has heard that Marcus is heavy into drugs again. His complexion looks unhealthy to Shelley. It'as obvious to her that he is on edge and very agitated.

Shelley manages to calm Marcus down enough to take his cell phone from him. Looking at his cell phone, Shelley notices that Marcus has had six missed calls from the same number.

Shelley dials the number. Marcus's sister and mother have been looking for him very urgently. Shelley speaks to Marcus's mother, as he isn't up to it. After finding out where Shelley and Marcus are, Marcus's sister is sent to pick them up. Marcus's father has committed suicide earlier the evening.

Shelley calls her parents the following day. Nick has empathy for the situation the family find themselves in, but asks Shelley not to become too involved with Marcus again.

This is the last comment she wants to hear from her father, but she knows from experience and their previous relationship that her father is right. Shelley has never told her parents though that she still has feelings for Marcus.

In the days that follow, Shelley supports Marcus and his family in their time of need. She explains to Nick that she can't just leave Marcus to struggle through this trying time in his life.

Marcus is dependent on her for his emotional well- being. Nick can see that it will not make any difference in the matter if he tries to explain to her that Marcus is using emotional psychology to his advantage to win Shelley back. It's shortly after becoming involved with Marcus again that Shelley's problems at work start.

She moves in with Marcus and his sister, who now share the townhouse of their deceased father. In so doing, Shelley no longer has the privilege of travelling to work with her colleague as she has before.

Shelley starts showing up late for work, or sometimes just doesn't go to work at all. The Director himself fires Shelley after two weeks of repetitive warnings which she pays no attention to.

Nick is furious, as is Constance, because Shelley is now living with Marcus, who also has no income. Amongst the two of them there is no money they can live off.

According to Marcus, his father's Life Insurance policy will be paying out very shortly, so there is no need for either him or Shelley to work. Nick supplies Shelley with the bare necessities to live, but he knows that Shelley will share everything with Marcus.

One month after the passing of Marcus' father, the life insurances pay out. Marcus and his sister have to vacate the townhouse prior to that. Having nowhere to go, Shelley turns to her parents for help. Marcus promises that it will only be for a short while before he finds himself another place to live.

He asks Nick for help in purchasing a vehicle, as he doesn't have much experience in doing so. Nick gives in and takes him to a car dealership, where he helps Marcus get a good deal by paying cash.

In the following two weeks after purchasing the car, Marcus and Shelley drive into the city every day, and return in the late afternoon. Money flows like water. Constance has an uneasy feeling, actually since Marcus and Shelley have started going to the city every day. Shelley has not been paying attention to her appearance lately.

This bothers Constance, as Shelley has always been very meticulous with her hair and make-up, and has also always dressed fashionably.

There are also dark smudges under Shelley's eyes. One afternoon she corners Shelley as well as Marcus when they arrive home. Constance comes straight to the point, not beating about the bush.

"Both of you, come here and sit down. There's something I'd like to speak to you about."

Shelley giggles like a school girl and slumps down on the sofa opposite Constance. She pulls Marcus down next to her. Marcus looks like he hasn't slept in days. His hair is disheveled and he appears jittery. Shelley speaks before Constance has a chance to say something.

"Oh my, this travelling to the city and back is exhausting!"

Shelley looks at Constance, and it's at that moment that she notices the distant look in Shelley's eyes. Her pupils are also enlarged.

"Shelley, what's wrong with the two of you?! You've taken something; what is it? Your eyes aren't focusing. I can see that you're high. Talk to me so we can help you!"

Shelley's answer is what Constance expects it would be.

"No mom, we're not doing drugs! Are you crazy to ask us something like that? How can you think so little of me?"

"Where have you been to everyday for the past two weeks, Shelley? I've noticed the change in your behavior, and your appearance has deteriorated. Don't lie to me!"

"Mom, we've been looking for a place to stay in the city. We actually found a nice little spot today, and we're moving in tomorrow. Sorry to lay it on you in such a hurry, but if we don't move in tomorrow we'll lose the place. It's cheap and it includes water and electricity."

Constance is caught off-guard by this sudden news flash of Shelley, and knows that she is lying about the drugs. Constance has a sickening feeling in her gut, but has no proof to prove otherwise.

The drug will wear off in a while, and apart from their physical appearance, there is nothing else to go on. Constance is busy turning all this over in her mind when Shelley and Marcus excuse themselves.

Each goes into their respective rooms and shut the doors. Con-stance talks to Nick when he arrives home from work, and tells him about the incident earlier that afternoon. Nick doesn't say much, but Constance knows that he will consider all angles of the situation before deciding on the best route to take.

Constance prepares dinner but neither Shelley, nor Marcus make their appearance. Nick instructs Constance not to dish up for either one.

"If they don't want to join us for dinner, that's their loss. They'll be good and hungry tomorrow morning. By the way, my girl, we'll be going with Shelley and Marcus to the city tomorrow to have a look at their place of residence. I don't care whether they like it or not, I'm not just going to take it lying down. They're both getting a piece of my mind."

xxx

During the time that Shelley has been living with Marcus again, Nick and Constance have maybe seen her once or twice, and hardly ever spoken to her on her cell phone. Shelley has let them know however, that she has landed a job at a liquor store outlet.

Nick knows the owner of the liquor store to be an honest and sincere man, as does Constance. They feel better for knowing that Shelley works for him.

A MINOR ADDICT

5 November 2012.

Constance and Nick receive a call from Shelley asking them whether she is welcome to return home. Shelley doesn't want to talk on the phone but adds that she will tell them everything when they go to pick her up.

Nick and Constance go through the following day, and when they arrive at Shelley's workplace to pick her up, the owner, who was in the Police force years before, calls Nick and Constance one side.

According to him Shelley needs help before it's too late. He has a feeling that she is on some kind of drug and needs rehabilitation, and getting Shelley away from Marcus is a definite prerequisite.

Shelley calls both her parents to the back of the liquor store when she goes for a smoke break outside.

"Mom, dad, I have a problem. I've been using drugs with Marcus since we went to live with you after his father passed away. That's why we came to the city every day; to buy the drugs. It's a new drug called Nyaope. We've been evicted from the place where we moved into two months ago, and lost everything we had. Actually, Marcus and myself have been pawning our stuff to buy more and more drugs. I've been missing work and suffering from time-lapses. My days have gaps in them that I can't recall. I'm afraid; please take me home and help me."

*Nyaope, or Whoonga:

This is the drug of choice amongst youngsters, and only available in South Africa. The reason for the choice of this drug is intertwined in the symbolism and uncertainty about a future that holds little or no hope for the prospect of gainful employment.

The explanation for the use of this or any other drug for that matter, is utter rubbish, of course, as anyone in their right mind will tell you.

In a world where your employment status determines what kind of white powder you consume, Nyaope finds itself at the bottom of the pile. It's an off-white powder, the core ingredients of this drug is a powerful mixture of Crystal Meth, Heroin and Marijuana. The Heroin is low-grade quality and cut with anything from rat poison to chlorine.

<u>*Pure Heroin:</u>

Is a white powder with a bitter taste, and is an Opiate. The color may vary to dark brown due to impurities left from the manufacturing process or the presence of additives.

Opiates are derived from Opium, which is in turn derived from the seeds of the poppy plant. Heroin is three times more potent than Morphine, and has a more direct route to the brain.

<u>Other names for heroine are:</u>

1. Smack.
2. Junk.
3. Thai White.
4. Jive.

Heroin is 1)mostly injected. However, high-purity heroin 2)can also be sniffed or smoked. It is also sometimes used in conjunction with other drugs, but far less often than a substance like dagga. It is usually heated on tin foil over an open flame, so that it liquefies. It is then injected.

The purity of heroin varies greatly.

<u>Heroin can be mixed with a great variety of damaging and lethal additives like:</u>

1. Powdered milk
2. Sugar
3. Baking soda
4. Procaine
5. Laundry detergent
6. Talc
7. Starch
8. Curry powder
9. Ajax cleaner
10. Strychnine. All of these additives are dangerous if they are injected into the bloodstream.

Heroin is smoked or inhaled as a powder or it can be mixed with water, heated, and then injected. Heroin crosses through the blood brain barrier 100 times faster than morphine since it is highly soluble in lipids.

Injecting heroin into a vein (intravenous use) produces effects in four to eight seconds. Injecting heroin into a muscle (intramuscular use) or under the skin (subcutaneous use) can produce effects in five to eight minutes.

Addicts sometimes inject themselves up to four times in one day. The needle marks in the groin, the elbows, the neck and so-called pocket shots (injected between the toes in order to avoid detection) are usually instant telltale marks that someone is using heroin.

Heroin depresses the central nervous system. It makes people feel intensely relaxed and causes a sensation of warmth and contentment. Heroin locks onto the body's endorphin receptors and mimics the body's feel-good hormones, called endorphins.

<u>The symptoms of heroin use include:</u>

1. Mood swings.
2. Personality changes.
3. Dilated pupils.
4. Changes in weight and general appearance.
5. For the worse; slurred speech.
6. Decreased sex drive.
7. Retarded social and emotional development.

It's easy to overdose on heroin as the strength of the drug is uncertain. It can lead to unconsciousness and respiratory failure.

<u>Heroin Detoxification.:</u>

Heroin causes dramatic withdrawal symptoms–much more dramatic than even strong drugs such as: Cocaine. About ten hours after the last heroin use, an addict's eyes begin to water and general flu-like symptoms are experienced.

<u>These include:</u>

1. Sneezing.
2. A feeling of weakness and depressions.
3. Muscle cramps.
4. Nausea
5. Vomiting
6. Diarrhea.

These symptoms can increase in severity over a period of two to three days.

These symptoms can take up to ten days to disappear and during this time, muscle spasms, violent shivering and cold chills are experienced. The latter gives its name to the detoxification process called 'cold turkey' as the skin resembles that of a plucked fowl.

A MINOR ADDICT

<u>Preparation of Nyaope:</u>

To ingest or smoke Nyaope, it must first be prepared. This is done in the following manner. The powder is put onto a shard of clean broken glass. A matching piece of glass is placed on top of the powder, which acts as a grinder. The fingers of each hand hold the pieces of glass together, while the wrists swivel back and forth until the powder reaches a fine state.

Meanwhile, a piece of cigarette paper and cannabis or dagga, are prepped. The powder is meticulously dusted off the glass to fall alongside the line of cannabis and rolled up, the edges licked to seal the paper. It can also be used by heating the ingredients and inhaling the smoke. Using this drug just once is enough to get hooked on it.

<u>The overall appearance after using Nyaope:</u>

<u>Users are generally:</u>

1. Glassy-eyed.
2. Reclusive.
3. Cliquey.

Smoking this drug gives them a sense of "power" to take on the days challenges of finding enough money to afford their next "hit."

Initially users feel euphoric, and when used in heavier doses, relaxed. However, the effects soon wear off and another hit is required. Less pleasant side effects include a severe painful stomach, muscle cramps and generally just feeling really ill.

When these symptoms ease up however, they use again. When using Nyaope, users can go for days without eating. This weakens their immune system and makes them susceptible to infections.

<u>Withdrawal is very harrowing and includes:</u>

1. stomach cramps.
2. Insomnia.
3. Diarrhea.
4. Vomiting.

Shelley starts crying and clings tightly to Constance, who also starts wiping away her own tears. Nick feels a lump in his throat and has to swallow hard to keep his emotions from taking over. He has to be strong for Constance; help Shelley get through this ordeal ...

"It'll be alright baby; don't worry about it. There is no reproach; we will beat this problem together. We're proud of you for having the courage to come forward and tell us about it. You've won half the battle already."

Nick hugs both the women in his life. There is nothing he will not do for them.

"Come on, let's go home. I'll get us KFC tonight, something you can bet Clark will be glad about."

They all laugh at this, as everybody knows how Clark loves chicken. It's his favorite food by choice.

Shelley resigned when she arrived at work that morning, and says her goodbyes now. Everybody is sad to see her leave. The owner gives Shelley her salary, as well as a little incentive bonus. Nick and Constance thank them for their help, and load Shelley's belongings into the car. Within a few minute's they are on their way. Shelley falls asleep on the rear seat.

On their arrival home, Clark is waiting for them. He gives Nick a hand unloading the suitcases and shakes his head. Nick sees this behavioral change in Clark, wondering what has brought this about.

"Clark, do you have something you'd like to say to me? I can see you're not happy with something."

Clark is taller than Nick and looks Nick squarely in the eyes when he replies "Yes, dad. I'm not happy with what's going on here", Clark retorts and points to the suitcases and Shelley. "Every time you and mom help her, and as soon as she feels like it, she kicks you right back in the teeth. She's laughing at the both of you, and using you for her own gain. She's back to make trouble, dad. Other than that, I'm only a spectator."

7 November 2012.

Two days after their arrival back home with Shelley she starts acting up. Her actions include sudden hysteria, aggressiveness and cold shivers.

During the past two days, Shelley doesn't eat much, and sleeps very little. She is nauseous and suffers from tremors since the previous afternoon. Her moods change as quickly as the seasons.

Shelley has started looking for trouble a little earlier on. A heated argument ensues between Nick and Shelley, and reaches boiling point.

"Shelley, what more do you want us to do to prove that we're willing to help you get through this ordeal? You are not making this easy on any of us!"

Shelley's eyes are wild as she screams "Stop being such a baby, daddy! All you do is whine and complain. Get some backbone, my goodness!"

Constance is appalled by the manner in which Shelley talks to Nick. The blood drains from Nick's face as he gets up from the couch.

"Shelley! Where do you get the audacity from to speak to your father in that manner after all he's done for you? If I ..."

"Drop it, mom! You're pathetic, do you know that? You never even complain about anything in your life; what's wrong, are you afraid dad will slap you around?"

Shelley laughs harshly. Nick's voice is like a whiplash.

"Shelley! That's enough; I won't tolerate you speaking to anyone of us like you're doing right now. What do you want from us? We've been trying to accommodate you and the lifestyle you've chosen for yourself to the best of our ability. None of us know who you are anymore!"

This tirade of Nick seems to have the effect it's meant to have, but not for long. Shelley is silent for a couple of seconds, then smiles a cold, vicious smile at both Nick and Constance.

"You rant and rave all day long about what this is doing to your life! Not once have you asked me how I feel, and why I do what I do. No; it's all about yourself! You have no compassion for my circumstances at all!"

Nick is at his wit's end, and throws his arms in the air out of hopelessness.

"You're not making anything easy, Shelley. The circumstances surrounding you are your own doing! Give us a bone here! I'm booking you into a rehab center on Monday and letting them address the problems you have. You can tell the Psychologists there your story. As far as I'm concerned, you've had a good life up to the time when you abandoned all your principles and let them fly out the window. I don't know what went wrong during your teenage years, but you seem to have gone off the path completely. You'd better sort out your priorities and be quick about it. Your life's a mess! I've had it with you!"

Shelley goes into a fit of rage and hysteria.

"I'm leaving right this minute! Don't try and stop me, because I'll call the police! I'm calling a friend to come and fetch me. The chances of any of you ever seeing me again, are zero. Do you hear me; zero! I hate you!"

Shelley storms out of the dining room and into her room. The door slams shut behind her. They hear cupboard doors open and bang shut. Everything becomes quiet after a few minutes, then Shelley darts out of her room and out the front door with her bags.

Nick and Constance run outside to call Shelley back, but she's already reached the corner of the block. A white Volvo skids to a halt beside her, and she quickly gets in. The car speeds off with screeching tires.

xxx

It's been six weeks since Shelley's dramatic disappearance; like the earth has swallowed her and she never existed. The situation has an overwhelming effect on Constance, who starts suffering from insomnia, headaches, depression and nightmares. Nick tries numerous times to get hold of Marcus' mother or sister; failing in his attempts to reach either one of them in order to achieve some clarification regarding Shelley's whereabouts.

CHAPTER EIGHT

Tuesday, 25 December 2012-10:00AM.

Nick and the rest of his family spend Christmas at his sister's house in the city. While they sit outside around a large table making small talk, Constance's cell phone rings.

She doesn't know the number, but answers it nonetheless. Nick sees a single tear roll from Constance's eye as she clasps her hand to her mouth. Her voice breaks.

"Shelley ...? Wha ... where are you? Yes; dad, Clark and I are spending the day here at Susan's house. Granny's also here. You want to see us? Sure, but don't you want to come here for a while; you're more than welcome to join us for Christmas lunch my angel. I'll tell daddy. Just wait there for us, we'll see you in a little while."

Constance is ecstatic when she hangs up. She calls Nick to one side. Her eyes are sparkling when she throws her arms around Nick's shoulders and says "Oh Nick! That was Shelley; she wants to see us! She asked whether we'd meet her at McDonald's by the new mall. Please Nick, I'm begging you. I know you might still be mad with her for the stunt she pulled last time, but if you could get it in your heart to forgive her ..."

"It's alright, my girl. I know how bad you want to see Shelley, and I'm not mad at her anymore. We'll go and meet her. But first, let's just tell the others to wait for us before they dish up."

Nick informs his sister and her husband about their plans.

"We'll be back in a little while. Come Clark, let's go and see Shelley, and find out how she's doing."

Constance convinces Nick to stop at another Mall first.

"Why, my girl? That's not even on the route we're supposed to take to where we should meet Shelley. I don't understand."

"Well, I thought we could buy Shelley a Christmas present as well. Not that she's expecting one, but it would be nice to give her something though, don't you think?"

Nick smiles and nods his head.

"You're always one jump ahead of me. It's an excellent thought, my girl. I hadn't thought of it. What would you like to buy her?"

Constance ponders this thought for a moment before she replies "Hmm, let me see. What about a nice watch; something lady-like? I know just what she'd like, and she doesn't have a watch."

When they arrive at McDonalds where Shelley is waiting for them, Constance is the first to exit the car. There is a girl sit-ting outside at one of the tables, and Constance walks right by her, opening the door to enter the fast food restaurant.

Entering, Constance lets her eyes roam the inside of the restaurant, expecting to see Shelley walk towards her. Instead, the girl sitting outside raps on the window. Nick looks for a second time and only then does he recognize Shelley. She is smiling, but Nick is shocked at what he sees.

Constance rushes outside when she sees that it's Shelley. Nick allows them a lot of time to hug and kiss. Tears spill and roll over both women's cheeks. At last Shelley walks hesitantly to Nick and looks up at him, searching his face with her eyes. Nick smiles and pulls her close into the circle of his arms, hugging her tight. She clings to him and cries.

"Daddy, I ..."

Nick silences her.

"Shh. No apologies, no reproach, Shell. We love you unconditionally."

They sit down at a table outside. Nick asks Shelley what she would like to order. At Shelley's request that they also have something, Constance replies that they are going to have a huge meal when they return to Susan's house.

Shelley hands Clark her order, and he goes inside the Diner to order it. Nick has been looking at Shelley while they are talking, and although she is friendly and seems happy, Nick can see and sense that something is amiss. She is wearing make-up, but Nick can see the blemishes on her skin underneath it.

There are dark circles underneath her eyes as well, although only slightly visible. Shelley's hair looks frizzled and unhealthy. Her hair has always had a healthy glow to it, and she always keeps her hair meticulously fashioned. As Nick sits opposite his daughter, he realizes that Shelley is only pretending. She looks unwell, and this bothers Nick immensely. He feels powerless, and angry for feeling this way.

"Shelley, are you doing alright? I mean, you're not ill or anything, are you?"

Shelley shakes her head from side to side, not looking at Nick or Constance when she answers. Her voice is barely audible.

"No daddy, I'm fine; really. It's good to see you guys again. Did you go to the South coast again this year? It's like tradition with you by now."

"Yes, we went there again, but it wasn't as good this year. There was quite a bit of rain, so we couldn't really do the things we usually used to do. I got pulled over by the traffic cops and fined five big ones. Fortunately, on the last day before we came back, I went to see the public Prosecutor. She laughed at my story, but reduced the fine to one hundred. Close call!"

Shelley laughs.

"I'll say! You're not used to being involved with the law; even with traffic fines and so on."

Shelley finishes her meal in no time at all, which makes Nick realize that she is hungry. She won't admit to it though, so Nick doesn't ask her. Shelley complains a lot during the conversation about stomach cramps.

Constance opens her handbag and hands Shelley a couple of tablets.

"Here, take this. It'll take the cramps away. You most probably ate too fast."

"I don't think so mom. I've been having a lot of stomach cramps lately, and nausea. Don't know what it is. It feels like I have flu. I'll go and see a doctor at the hospital some time or other and get some medication."

Constance leans closer and takes Shelley's hand.

"You're probably not eating healthy enough. Promise me you'll look at your eating habits. It'll make me feel much better, and let me know what the doctor says, will you?"

Shelley just shrugs her shoulders.

"Okay mom. I'll eat healthier foods, but I doubt whether it's going to make much of a difference with regards to the way I feel."

"Shelley, are you ... still taking the drugs you were on when we saw you the last time? I don't want to cause trouble; I just want to know."

"Nick, how can you ask her such a question? What if ..."

"It's alright mom. No, daddy, I'm not on drugs anymore."

"Where are you staying at the moment; are you back with Marcus?"

Shelley nods her head.

"Yes, I'm back with Marcus, and we're staying with a guy who's in a relationship with Marcus' mother. Neither me, nor Marcus is working at the moment, but at least we have a roof over our heads."

Nick leans over and strokes Shelley's arm.

"If you need help, baby, just ask. You know we're always there for you, don't you?"

Shelley wipes her eyes and nods her head. Her lips quiver when her voice comes out in a whisper.

"Yes daddy, I know. Thank you for always being there when I need you and mom. You don't know how much I appreciate it, even though I've caused so much trouble for you. That's my only anchor in life; knowing you're there when I need you."

Constance wipes away tears while Shelley speaks. Nick looks away, choking back the sob that is tearing his heart to pieces. There's an awkward silence for a while. Constance dries her tears and takes the present they bought for Shelley, from her handbag. Shelley's eyes grow wide with surprise and her face lights up when it's offered to her. Her smile is radiant after she opens and stares at it in awe. She gasps with delight.

"Oh, my goodness; this is so beautiful! Thank you so very much all of you. Unfortunately I couldn't get you anything, I'm sorry."

Constance and Nick reply simultaneously "There's no need to apologize, honey."

Nick hastily carries on talking.

"We didn't come here to collect presents; we came because we wanted to see you."

They converse for a couple of minutes more before Nick announces that they have to return for lunch. Constance takes some family photos, including everybody in them. Shelley smiles beautifully on each one. The goodbye is very emotional, leaving Constance as well as Shelley in tears, with Nick swallowing hard at the huge lump in his throat. His vision is blurry and his heart feels heavy and empty.

A MINOR ADDICT

Monday, 31 December 2012-1:15 PM.

Nick has just opened his car door, and is about to get into the driver's seat when he hears Constance's bloodcurdling scream from inside the house.

Nick scrambles out of the car and on his way out of the garage, when Constance enters, shouting and screaming hysterically. Nick tries to calm her down and find out what the problem is.

Constance sinks to the concrete floor while holding her head between her hands. She is trembling all over, and Nick shakes her once. Clark appears on the scene and looks bewildered.

"Constance! Tell me what's wrong; I can't make out a word you're saying. Be calm and start from the beginning."

Constance cries out, but is a little calmer.

"Nick, I just received a message that my father passed away fifteen minutes ago! How is that possible? We just spoke to him on Christmas day; now he's gone!"

Nick feels like he's been struck by lightning. Still in shock, he pulls Constance close and comforts her.

"Oh, my girl, I don't know what to say. That's just awful! How did it happen?"

"My sister says that he died from asphyxiation! I need to get there, Nick; as soon as possible! Will you take me?"

Nick helps Constance get upright.

"It's okay, my girl, we'll go to your mom's. I'm sure everybody will be there by the time we arrive. Clark, pack your overnight bag just in case."

Nick leads Constance inside and lets her lie down on the sofa to rest while he packs their suitcase to take with. He calls Shelley's number and after several rings, Shelley answers.

"Shelley, how are you doing, honey? I'm afraid I have bad news; Granddad has just passed away. I know it's very sudden. Yes, we're going through to Grandma's now. Can we come and pick you up on our way? Not? Okay, I'll tell Grandma and keep you informed of the developments. Keep well; we love you!"

Clark locks the house and sets the alarm while Nick packs their bags into the car. Within minutes they are on the road. He has given Constance a sedative, and she is calmer.

She dials her eldest sister's number, who answers immediately. They talk for a while, and Constance informs Nick that everybody is going to her sister's house, which is a three-hour drive.

They arrive at the house of Constance's sister at six thirty, just as dusk starts setting in. The entire family is present, and after much debating, Nick and Constance decide to stay overnight.

Both Nick and Clark try several times during the evening to contact Shelley, but she remains unavailable. They retire to bed just after midnight, leaving Constance and her sisters to talk about the funeral service of their deceased father.

A MINOR ADDICT

Tuesday, 1 January 2013; 08:00AM.

Nick receives a voice message on his cell phone. Listening to the voicemail, Nick has to listen carefully to distinguish Shelly's voice from that of the background noise. It's overbearingly loud. Nick hears that Shelley's speech is slurred when she leaves the message.

"Daddy; Happy New Year, you guys! I'm at a party as you can hear, and I'm foolishly drunk. Just wanted to tell you to come and pick me up on your way home. Call me when you're on your way, and I'll tell you where to pick me up. See you a little later!"

Nick goes to where Constance is preparing breakfast for them in the kitchen. She didn't sleep at all the previous night, and her eyes are a little puffy from crying and the lack of sleep.

"My girl, Shelley left a voice message on my cell, asking us to pick her up on our way back home. When we've finished our breakfast, we can hit the road. Clark has already loaded our suitcases into the car."

This news brings a smile to Constance's lips again amidst all the heartache that she's experienced since the previous day. After breakfast they thank Constance's eldest sister for her hospitality and depart.

As bad luck intends it to be, Murphy's Law plays along, and they could not get hold of Shelley that day or for a long time after that. Shelley did also not attend the funeral of her granddad the following week. Constance not only had to deal with the sudden death of her father, but also with the grief of a disinterested daughter at a time when she needs her support most.

Shelley disappears off the face of the earth, or so it seems. Nick goes to the police and reports Shelley as missing. The Police opens a docket and a detective is put in charge of her disappearance.

Constance and Nick dread every phone call. Calling the friends Shelley has in the city doesn't do anything to improve matters, as none of them have seen her in quite some time.

Constance suffers from insomnia and other stress-related health problems during this trying time. Nick can do nothing else but support her emotionally and psychologically.

207

A MINOR ADDICT

Six weeks later; 14 February 2013, 16:45PM. Nick arrives home from work, and is drinking his coffee Clark has made for him, when the broadcast is interrupted with an important bulletin.

"We have just received news that the South African blade runner Olympic gold medal winner, Oscar Pistorius, has shot and killed his fiancé, Miss Reeva Steenkamp, this morning. The incident took place in Oscar's town house at an upmarket Estate. Miss Steenkamp was pronounced dead at the scene when the Police arrived to investigate the shooting. She had been shot four times through the bathroom door. A cricket bat was also found on the scene with traces of blood and hair on it. It's not known at this time of the investigation what the bat was used for, although it is said that the weapon will be taken in for forensic tests. Oscar Pistorius has been arrested and will be detained until Monday morning when he will appear in the Magistrate's court and charged."

208

Nick has heard enough. He gets up, upset about the bulletin, and turns to Constance.

"Did you just listen to that? I'm telling you that guy's going to get away with just a slap on the wrist, because it's a high profile case. He has a lot of money, so he can afford the best Lawyers and Advocates money can buy, and he can also buy his way past the Judge when sentencing is done. I hate it when justice doesn't prevail. What about that poor girls' parents?"

Nick's cell phone rings. Out of habit more than anything else, Nick answers without looking at the number on his cell phone's screen. Constance sees Nick's body jerk as he puts down his coffee cup. "Shelley?! What..., where are you? Stop crying, I can't hear what you're saying. That's better, yes; now I can hear you."

"Daddy, please, can you come and fetch me? I'm going to take an overdose of drugs if you don't come! Please, I beg you; come and fetch me! I can't do this anymore; I've had enough of this kind of life!"

Shelley's voice is shrill with hysteria, and Nick can hear by the tone in her voice that she is close to breaking point. There is a moment of silence before Nick answers, as a thought enters his mind. As quickly as the thought enters his mind, Nick brushes it aside. Shelley needs their help!

"Yes, we'll be there, Shelley. Where are you? Yes, I remember where that is. Just wait there; don't go anywhere, we'll see you in about an hour!"

Constance jumps up and races closer to Nick, her eyes filled with countless questions. She bursts out crying when she hears Nick's explanation regarding Shelley's call.

"Nick, let's leave at once! Where did she say she was?"

Nick holds up his hands to stop the torrent of words that he knows will follow.

"It's going to be alright, my girl. Don't worry, we'll go and get her; I know where she is. I'm just not sure how long she'll stay put, so let's hit the road! Clark, lock the doors; let's get going."

Within minutes the Callahan's are on their way to meet Shelley and bring her home. Arriving at the place where Shelley said she would be waiting on them, there is at first no sign of her. Nick has a hollow, nauseating feeling on the pit of his stomach when the thought that they have once again been had, strikes him. He doesn't relay this thought to Constance. Instead, he calls Shelley's number. After a couple of rings, Shelley answers.

"Daddy, are you here already? Thank heavens! I was beginning to think that you weren't going to show! I'm inside the estate; I'll be out in a couple of minutes. Wait for me in front of the main entrance."

"We'll be waiting right here, honey."

Upon Constance's questions regarding their conversation, Nick answers that Shelley is on her way out to meet them in a couple of minutes.

They wait patiently for her arrival.

Just as Nick startx growing uncomfortable and impatient, he catches a glimpse of movement at the entrance to the Estate. Shelley appears and walks quickly towards the car. Without hesitation, she opens the rear passenger door and slides in next to Clark.

In one smooth motion she closes the door. Nick makes a quick observation, and thinks that someone or something has put a huge scare into Shelley. She interrupts Nick's thoughts. There is urgency in her voice.

"Daddy, can you please just start the car and go? I'll greet you properly when we get home. For now I just want to get away here."

Nick is startled, but does as Shelley asks. He looks at Shelley in the rear-view mirror.

"Where are your clothes, Shelley? I thought you had everything here."

"No, daddy; my clothes aren't with me. I left everything at the place where I've been staying in a garage for quite some time now. I'm leaving it all behind; there's still a lot of my clothes at home, so don't worry. Just head home, please."

On the way home, Constance tries to make conversation with Shelley, but it doesn't go well. Shelley is quiet and wants to be left alone. She complains about not feeling very well, and sounds bad; like she has a cold or the flu.

Halfway home, Shelley falls asleep. The silence that ensues until they enter their home town is a peaceful one, each of them tied up with their own thoughts.

The time is eight o'clock when Nick opens the gate to their driveway. He lets Constance and Clark out to unlock the front door while he parks the car in the garage and helps Shelley into the house. Constance prepares something quick to eat, but Shelley refuses to have anything to eat.

She admits to Nick and Constance that she has started withdrawing from the drugs around the same time that she made the call to Nick's cell phone. Upon questioning her, they find out that she has had her last "fix" late that morning.

Shelley starts crying and complains that her muscles are aching. She is also shivering and has goose bumps all over her body. Inside the house, Nick has a good look at Shelley, and is shocked at her appearance.

He knows instinctively that she has to receive medication, otherwise she will end up keeping them awake all night and they'd all be worse off in the morning. Shelley is given a strong sedative, and before long her eyes are heavy with sleep. The sedative knocks her out cold until the following morning.

xxx

Friday, 15 February 2013. Everybody in the Callahan household is up and about. Nick calls his supervisor to take a leave of absence from work, explaining that Shelley needs to get medical attention very urgently.

Constance calls the family Physician and is fortunate to get an appointment for Shelley at one o' clock the afternoon. Shelley has been left to sleep until she awakes on her own. She looks worse than the previous evening and doesn't want anything to eat. She is pale and off balance. Nausea overcomes Shelley twice before they leave for her appointment.

The physician does a thorough examination, and informs Nick and Constance to book Shelley into a rehabilitation center immediately. She has all the signs of withdrawing from Heroin and other related substances.

The Physician explains that if Shelley does not receive help fast, the danger of her going into shock is definite. The doctor gives them a couple of contact numbers for private as well as government institutions who come highly recommended for substance abuse rehabilitation.

Before leaving the physician's consultation room, the sister injects Shelley with a strong sedative to help her with the worst withdrawal symptoms until she is admitted at a rehab center.

After contacting several of the recommended institutions, Nick and Constance decided on one in the neighboring State. It's far, but Shelley needs to go somewhere where nobody can reach her, neither knows her.

Shelley has only this one time to start afresh, and seeing that she is in no condition to make important choices, it's their duty as parents to fulfil this obligation. Nick drives to a clothing store where Constance purchases new clothes for Shelley to take with her to the rehab center.

He also has to do an electronic fund transfer to the full amount of the costs involving Shelley's treatment, which is a substantial amount of money. At four o' clock they are on their way to the rehabilitation center, with Shelley lying quietly on the back seat, totally oblivious to her surroundings for the moment.

Nick pulls into the parking area at the rehabilitation center in front of the main entrance twenty minutes before check-in time is about to expire. After filling out forms, After Shelley is admitted, she is taken to her room, where Constance helps her unpack her belongings.

A security guard appears and searches Shelley's bags and closet, and satisfied that there are no illegal substances brought in, declares the "zone" safe.

A sister enters Shelley's room and informs Shelley and her parents that she will be locked in the room for a period of three days without any contact from outside, including telephone calls.

They also deny Shelley any contact with other patients during this time, and she will have room service during this period. The sister explains that Shelley will be given time to "dry out" during this three-day period.

It is called the "Cold Turkey" phase. Upon further enquiry by Nick about the "drying out" phase of the first three days, they are taken into the sister's office where she explains the procedure to them.

"Mister and missus Callahan, we'll be giving Shelley two injections in the morning after breakfast. The first injection is a B-co injection, which comprises of a selection of the best vitamin B's available, and includes vitamin B12. These vitamins will boost her immune system. She gets the second injection three times daily during the first three days' she is kept in confinement. It's a 20 milligram Valium injection, and serves to keep her calm. It also helps with the withdrawal of the toxins in her body. After she comes out of confinement, she will still receive her vitamin B-co injections. We will reduce the Valium's dosage to 10 milligram twice daily for the next seven days. After seven days we will take her off all medication."

It sounds almost too good to be true to Nick. Nick finds it hard to believe that the detoxification process from the extreme substances will only take ten days to clear from Shelley's organs and body.

"Excuse me for sounding a little sceptic sister, but do you mean to tell me that that will be the only help she is going to receive, and that she will then be cured from her addiction? I find that very hard to believe."

The sister smiles and calmly replies "Well, mister Callahan, it's not only the medication which they receive that speeds up the recovery process, but also the Therapeutic treatment we provide in conjunction with the medication every day. They have one-on-one therapy sessions as well as group sessions every day until two o' clock in the afternoon. When they have completed their sessions for the day, they are given "home-work" to complete for the next session. Part of the therapy is called Cognitive therapy, where they are taught to control the urge to relapse in a Psychological manner."

Nick and Constance are impressed with the level of professional ethics the rehabilitation center is run with. The sister continues with her short educational lesson.

"After Shelley is released from our rehab, there are follow-up sessions for a period of two years. This includes a session with her therapist once a month for the first six months, there after once every three months and finally once every six months. The parents or life-partners are included in these after-care sessions to ensure that they have the knowledge to keep the ex-addict from relapsing. Our aim is to change their way of thinking, and we're successful eight out of ten times. I hope our way of treatment gives you peace of mind."

Constance nods her head.

"Thank you for the information you've shared with us, sister. We're satisfied that Shelley will be getting the kind of treatment necessary for her to overcome the addiction."

The sister rises to her feet and comes around her desk. She shakes their hands and smiles.

"I'm glad that you're satisfied. Your daughter will be a totally different person when you see her again, that's a promise. After the initial confinement period of three days, Shelley will be allowed to receive visitors during the week on Tuesday and Thursday and of course, every weekend from then on in."

This explanation helps the Callahan's understand the purpose of the treatment. The sister gives the Callahan's time alone with Shelley before their departure. Constance and Shelley both cry a lot.

For the following three days Nick and Constance call the rehabilitation center at intervals to find out how Shelley has been doing since they've left her there. The feedback is always the same. The staff tell Nick and

Constance that Shelley is doing well under the circumstances, and that she should be given the three days "drying-out" time to flush her system from the toxins of her lifestyle.

CHAPTER NINE

Tuesday, 19 February 2013; 4:30PM.

The Callahan's have just arrived at the rehab center for their visit with Shelley. She has come out of her three day isolation period that morning, and calls Constance immediately.

A staff member shows them into the visitor's lounge where they can wait for Shelley to be called. Shelley enters the lounge quietly and stands there for a moment before announcing her arrival. She clears her throat and smiles radiantly.

"Hi, everybody. I've waited sooo long to see you guys!"

She runs into Nick's arms and buries her face in his shirt, sobs tearing with raw emotion from her petite figure. Nick holds her in his embrace until her emotions are under control. Shelley steps back and walks to Constance, hugging her for a long time before she also does the same with Clark. She holds her head high and speaks with a faint smile plucking at the corners of her lips.

"Let's go and get some fresh air, you guys. I have a lot to tell you!"

Leading the way, Shelley takes her parents and brother out into the garden, where several other youngsters are sitting around on benches. They go to sit on a bench a ways from all the other patients.

Shelley lights a cigarette and offers Constance one as well. Nick had seen immediately when Shelley had entered the visitor's lounge that there is a change in her attitude.

"Mom, dad, I can't tell you how good I feel again for the first time in years! My mind's clear, and I can actually think for myself; something I haven't been able to do for a long time. I'm still a little shaky, but it'll disappear within the next two weeks or so. Oh yes, my skin feels a little creepy, but I'm coping. We had dinner just before you arrived, and I ate a lot. It felt so good to be able to eat again. You have no idea how long I went without food while I was doing drugs. I'm so ashamed of myself, and I can't stand the thought of how disappointed you all are in me! If only I could turn back time!"

Constance puts her arm around Shelley's shoulders. "Honey, we all make mistakes. We're not disappointed in you; we're disappointed with the decisions you made. All of us are immensely proud of you for taking the first step to overcome your dependency. You helped yourself! That shows that you have courage and determination to succeed. Oh honey, we're just so grateful that you came out of this alive! We spent countless hours praying for your well-being, and it was well worth it in the end."

A tear rolls down Constance's cheek. Nick can see that she finds it difficult to keep her composure. Shelley takes Constance's hand in hers and caresses it.

"I'm so grateful that my life was spared, mom. Even more so; I've been given the opportunity to re-unite with my family and clear my slate."

Constance acknowledges this fact by nodding her head.

"We're all very grateful that it worked out this way, honey. It could so easily have turned out differently."

Nick clears his throat.

"What is the staff like, Shelley? Do you have a lot of free time during the day, or is most of your time taken up by therapy sessions?"

Shelley shakes her head in denial.

"No, daddy, we don't actually have time to loaf around here. The only time we get to relax a little, is during lunch hour and tea-break in the afternoon, and then of course when we've finished our daily routine of therapy sessions. Other than that, we're busy with group session therapy and one-on-one sessions with our therapists. I actually had my first session today."

"And ...?"

"Oh, it wasn't too bad. It was quite enlightening as a matter-of-fact. I found out a number of things that I never knew before, things I blamed myself for. I'll tell you all about it at a later stage, though. At the moment I'm not exactly confident enough to talk about it yet."

"That's alright, honey; we understand. What else can you tell us?"

Shelley smiles brightly, her eyes shining with excitement.

"If everything goes well and I show improvement, I get to come home for the weekend in two weeks' time. Isn't that super-cool? I can't wait!"

They all agree that it definitely is something to look forward to. Clark asks something that he's been dying to ask since they have arrived.

"Hey Shell, how's the food here; is it at least edible?"

It's completely off the topic of the conversation, and makes everybody laugh. Shelley enjoys Clark's wisecrack immensely.

"To answer your question; the food's actually quite good. We order our meals from a menu every morning. We had dinner just before you arrived, and had hamburgers and French fries with a salad."

Clark is impressed.

"That sounds great! I could do with a burger right about now."

They all laugh and enjoy the rest of their visit. Clark tells tales from the past that brings very pleasant memories back. It is with heavy hearts that they depart when early evening comes. They promise to call every night, and to visit when the weekend arrives. The Callahan's ride back feeling light-hearted and very pleased. Constance voices everybody's opinion.

"Shelley looks good, doesn't she? It's been years since I've seen her this way. Oh, Nick, I'm so grateful for the second chance she's received! There are so many people who aren't fortunate enough to get the help they need, and as a result of that they're outcasts in society. I feel so sorry for them! Everybody deserves a second chance at a good life."

Nick nods his head.

"I agree, my girl. The other thing to remember is that not everyone wants a second chance, even when they're presented with one. Many addicts don't want to break the habit of addiction, because they're so far gone that they can't live without their "fix." Countless addicts die or find themselves admitted to Psychiatric institutions when the drugs get taken from them. We are very blessed."

Over the following three weeks Shelley's improvement is amazing, and when it's time for her to check out of the rehab center and go home, she has become so positive in her attitude towards substance abuse, that she can talk about it without any discomfort.

Life is good. Everything in their lives return to normal after Shelley's rehabilitation. The Callahan's can't believe that they have survived the trying times they've been put through. It's like a vague memory that has never existed.

Shelley lands herself an interesting job at a photographic one-hour lab. Fortunately, her previous experience with the designing company in the city counts in her favor.

She is the only employee at the photo lab who can work with the latest programs. Three and a half months later trouble looms its ugly head into the Callahan household once more.

xxx

Monday; 15 July 2013, 1:15PM.

Nick's cell phone rings incessantly, with an almost urgent sound to it. The sound startles Nick, as he is thinking about the last couple of months since Shelley's rehabilitation and how blessed they have been since then. It's like life has dealt them a new deck of cards to play with. He sees that it's Shelley and answers with a smile.

"Hello, pretty little lady! How has your day been up to now?"

When Shelley speaks, Nick can hear that she is highly upset.

"Daddy, I'm resigning from this job right this minute! My employer and his mother have falsely accused me of some things that never happened, and it's not the first time this has happened. I'm not going to take their insults any longer! Write me a letter of resignation so I can hand it in please. Just e-mail it to me; I'll print it here at the photo lab and sign it before I hand it in."

Nick felt a stab of alarm as he listens to Shelley's tirade.

"Honey, calm down and tell me what's happened. Don't be hasty and make bad decisions you'll regret later on. Let's talk this over when you come home from work."

Shelley, however, is adamant in her decision.

"Daddy, I've already made up my mind. Nothing you or anybody else says will convince me otherwise. That's fine; if you don't want to write me a letter of resignation, I'll just leave without one! I'll walk home as well!"

"Hang on Shelley; I'll e-mail the letter to you right away. Are you going to complete today's shift?"

There is a short silence at Shelley's end.

"Uhm ... no, I'm leaving right after I hand in my resignation, daddy. Can you come and pick me up, or should I walk home?"

Nick hangs his head in despair. Just when it starts looking like everything is back on track; this had to happen! Nick sighs loudly. He is devastated, and knows from past experiences that there is something else behind the story.

"Look Shelley, you'll have to wait until I leave work. I can't just leave here to pick you up. I'm busy at the moment, so you'll just have to wait it out for now. I'll see you after four. I'll mail you the resignation letter in the meantime."

Nick hangs up and quickly writes the letter. At four o' clock, Nick drives straight to Shelley's work. On his arrival, he finds Shelley waiting for him outside. Nick has hardly stopped the car, before Shelley slides into the passenger seat and asks Nick to drop her off at a friend's house.

"Daddy, just drop me at Beth's house, please. I don't feel like going home right at this minute. Beth's father will take me home a little later on tonight."

Nick isn't sure whether this is such a great idea, but he doesn't want to cause unnecessary arguments. He sees by Shelley's demeanor that she will snap back at him. Nick voices his opinion, however when he says "Shelley, I don't know what happened, but I do think that you acted before thinking it through. It's a little late now, but never make any decisions which might have an impact on your life when you're angry. Ones' perception of things is a lot clearer when your mind is calm. There is one other thing; when you come home later tonight, we're going to have a discussion about what happened at your work. Mom and I would like to know. Maybe there's something we can do to diffuse the situation, huh?"

Looking at her out of the corner of his eye, Nick sees Shelley bite her lower lip and roll her eyes at him. He knows the signs. Shelley will try to get time on her side by coming home late, hoping that the discussion can be avoided. Nick is also adamant though, to pursue the matter before it can escalate to cause bigger problems later on.

"Alright daddy, that's fine by me. We'll talk when I get home, alright? There's nothing to tell really; it's just that I'm tired of being accused of things that I don't do. I can't work somewhere if I'm not trusted, now can I? I don't think you'd enjoy working in such conditions."

Nick realizes that he has tightened his grip around the steering wheel. His knuckles are white.

"Shelley, this isn't about me, and there has to be a reason why you always get into trouble just as soon as things start going right. Here we are; go and ask Beth if her father will be taking you home. I'll wait for you to come and tell me, otherwise I'll fetch you at seven o' clock."

Shelley is gone for a couple of minutes before she returns.

"Beth says it's alright, dad. Her father will take me home, so don't worry; we'll have our little talk tonight. Thank you for picking me up at work; see you later."

Nick starts his car and heads home to inform Constance about the situation at hand.

xxx

Later that night; the Callahan household. Shelley arrives home in time for dinner. After dinner, the Callahan's sit down in the dining room to hear what Shelley has to say. Clark asks to be excused, as he doesn't want to take part in the proceedings.

He goes to his room and closes the door, as he plans to play his guitar. Constance starts the conversation.

"Shelley, dad told me what happened today. This all seems a bit out of the ordinary. Everything was going so well these past couple of months, and now this. What happened, and why did you resign?"

Shelley, who has been a little uneasy since arriving home, knows that there is no way out of this predicament for her. She steels herself and takes a deep breath, sighing as she does so.

There is a moment's silence before Shelley's voice breaks the uncomfortable atmosphere that hangs in the air after Constance's question.

"Mom, dad, I'm going to tell you the story exactly the way it happened. Just before I was about to go on lunch one of the guys who was also in the rehab center with me, came into the shop. It's Malawi, the Nigerian who stays just outside of town. I was busy with a client, so he stood to one side, and we started talking. When he left, Jeff called me into his office. His mother, who has never liked me, was also present. She told Jeff that Malawi gave me a small package and I apparently stuffed this into my bra. Well, it's needless to say that he believed his mother's story, even though I said that it wasn't true. Jeff gave me two options. He said that I could either resign, or he would call the cops on me and have me arrested. Should I decide to resign, he would pay me the salary he owed me, otherwise I wouldn't get anything. That's why I resigned."

Nick looks at Constance and shakes his head.

"Shelley, that's unfair dismissal. He isn't allowed to do that, and you shouldn't have let him push you into a corner. That's why I asked you to first discuss it with me. Now you've resigned for no obvious reason, and you're without a job again. It doesn't make sense! You should have called his bluff. Does he have any other proof of what he says you did besides what he heard from his mother? If he doesn't, he's in big trouble according to the employment act. I'll take you to the Labor Department tomorrow morning; how about that?" Shelley vehemently shakes her head.

"No daddy, rather leave this whole sordid affair. Drop it; I'll rather look for another job, which won't be so difficult to find. Jeff said that I could go and collect my salary the day after tomorrow, and that's what I intend doing. I'm sorry about all the drama, but like I said; it's not worth fighting over."

Nick shakes his head and holds up his hands.

"Now that's where you're wrong, Shelley. This is your name that's being dragged through the mud, and it will precede you into the future."

Shelley is immovable in her decision.

"I don't want to argue about it any longer, or discuss it. I've made up my mind, and that's all there is to it. Let's just move on and put this behind us, please you guys. I'm going to draw myself a nice hot bath before I go to bed. Goodnight!"

After Shelley leaves Nick and Constance, they look at each other in utter disbelief. They can't believe that Shelley is so cool and calm about the entire situation. Something doesn't feel right to Nick, but he doesn't want to meddle in Shelley's business. He voices his concern to Constance though, as they always share their feelings and are honest with one another.

"My girl, I'm not so sure that everything happened exactly the way Shelley wants us to believe it did. It sounds like there are some blank spots in her story. I don't know; maybe I'm just being prejudiced, but I'm not happy with what she has told us. Are you happy?"

Constance shrugs her shoulders.

"Nick, I feel the same way you do, but it's no use pointing fingers. Let's wait it out and see what happens, alright? If she wants some breathing space, let's give it to her. I hope you're mistaken, for all our sake's."

Nick ponders on this for a moment before answering.

"Yes, I suppose you're right. I could well be acting a little paranoid. It's just that this has happened so many times before when she was in the city, that I fear the worst when I hear things like this. It feels like an electric current running through my body when I hear that Shelley's in trouble, and there's no way of cutting the switch, because everything just snow-balls from there on out! I sound insane to myself."

Constance smiles at Nick's portrayal of things and replies "You might be going a little overboard, but I can understand it. She's supposed to be daddy's little girl, and in your circle of protection. Sadly, she hasn't been that for a very long time, my darling, and I know how you miss that.

Don't think that I haven't noticed the tears well up when we watch a movie where a father and daughter scene is involved."

Nick smiles when he listens to Constance explain his feelings. He never knew that Constance is aware of how he feels. His heart throbs wildly when he thinks of the possibility that trouble may be looming ahead. Nick doesn't want to infuse any negative thoughts, but he has a nagging, uneasy feeling that won't let go of him ...

xxx

Wednesday, 17 July 2013.

Shelley leaves the house at 11:00AM to collect her salary from Jeff, her ex-employer. By three o' clock the afternoon, neither Nick nor Constance have received any news from Shelley. She has promised both her parents that she will give them a call a little later on, as she plans to go shopping for a few things she needs.

Nick calls Shelley's number a few times, but has no luck. Her cell phone diverts to her voice mailbox, where Nick leaves messages for her to call back. Arriving home after work, Nick learns that Constance and Clark also tried to get hold of Shelley. Neither of them have had any luck either. Constance is a nervous wreck by the time dusk sets in. Nick is not any better. Clark holds the fort, and prepares a light dinner for them.

"Mom, dad, I think Shelley's just having a bit of fun. I'm sure she'll show up or contact one of us a little later on."

"Thank you, Clark, but I have a feeling we won't be hearing from her tonight, son. Why has her phone been unavailable all day long? You know how your sister feels about her phone. No, this is something else, Clark. If we haven't heard from her by tomorrow morning early, I'm filing a missing person's report. I'm calling the police right now just to make sure what the time-limit is on filing a missing person's report."

Constance is quiet up to this point in time. She is in a state of shock and can not believe, as does Nick, that Shelley is doing this to them again.

"Yes please, Nick; call the police and find out how long we have to wait before they'll respond to someone who is reported as missing. I can't take this Nick; not again. It feels like the time when she was in the city, and we had no idea of where she was. If only she'd call us and tell us where she is, and when she'll be back, but to not be available; it's driving me insane!"

Nick sits Constance down on the sofa and lets her lie back.

"Don't worry, my girl. We'll get this sorted out. You just lie back and close your eyes for a while. I'll get Clark to make us a nice cup of tea in the meantime."

Nick turns to Clark, who is busy on his cell phone.

"Clark, would you mind getting us something to drink? I think mom will have some hot cocoa, and I'll have some decaffeinated coffee, please."

Clark puts his cell phone down.

"Sure dad; no problem. I also feel like some coffee."

Nick calls the local police station, and at his question on what the timeframe is before someone can be reported as missing, he is told that it's twenty-four hours. Disgustedly Nick disconnects the call, a scowl on his face.

"A person could be lying in a ditch by the time they decide to start looking! They really have some ridiculous policies that need urgent revision. The Policeman says because Shelley's of age, she could be visiting with friends, and is entitled to her privacy. According to him it's not for us to say that she's in any kind of danger at the moment. He reckons if she doesn't shown up by eight o' clock tomorrow morning, we can file a missing person's report. What a jerk!"

Sleep is out of the question and the night drags by very slowly. Nick takes a few catnaps during the night for a couple of minutes, and is exhausted when dawn's misty grey fingers break through the dark veil of night.

He drinks several mugs of coffee, and works on his laptop, which keeps him going for the most part. Constance sleeps for a couple of hours, but is restless most of the time while she is asleep. Nick decides to be at the police station very early in order to get all the paper work done.

xxx

Thursday, 18 July 2013. The officer who opens a missing person's report on Shelley is very helpful. It doesn't take long to complete the docket, and the report goes out to all patrol cars to be on the lookout for Shelley. Each patrol car receives a full description of Shelley on their on-board computers as well as a recent photo.

The officer assures Nick that a patrol car will pick Shelley up as soon as they spot her. They prioritize her disappearance as a high profile case. Nick thanks him and leaves the police station.

Calling Constance, Nick explains to her what has happened since he has left home a while ago. Satisfied that they are at least now searching for Shelley, Nick discloses that he wants to go around to Shelley's work where she resigned two days previously.

It's Nick's theory that someone there may know something that can be of help in the search. Entering the place of business, Nick asks to speak to Shelley's ex-employer. He invites Nick into his office and sits down behind his desk.

"Please take a seat, mister Callahan. How can I be of service to you?"

"Thank you, Jeff. This is an awkward situation. I'd just like to know what happened here on Monday, because I think it's relevant to what is happening now. Did you know that Shelley has been missing since yesterday after she came here to collect her salary? Did anyone here see her get into a car with someone? Could you please find out for me? The police are searching for her as we speak, and I'd be grateful for any other information we might be able to gather which would help us find her."

Shelley's ex-employer is shocked to hear this and shakes his head.

"I was not aware of this, mister Callahan; I'm sorry. Let's go to the front and find out if one of my staff knows something."

Jeff calls his staff one by one to find out whether they know something. Two of the staff recall an incident. They discuss it before one of them answers.

"Yes, we remember the guy who was here with her. He had dark brown, spiky hair, and he was quite tall. The car he arrived in, was quite old as well, and he parked it across the street. It was a white car, but we can't remember what the make of it was. Shelley just took her salary and didn't say much to any of us. She still said she was going to go shopping, turned around and left with that guy. She never introduced him to us, so we can't tell you what his name is. Hang on a minute; a while back there was another man who came here quite a lot. He also had spiky hair, although it's not the same guy. She never introduced any of them to us."

Nick thanks them and turns to Jeff.

"Thank you. It's not much to go on, but I'll share the information with the police. They might be able to do something with it."

Jeff calls Nick one side.

"Mister Callahan, I don't know whether Shelley has told you what happened here on Monday. I don't want to speak out of turn, but I would also not like you to think of me as the culprit here. I acted in good faith, and it was not a light decision I made on the spur-of-the moment. It was due to happen sometime or other."

This statement shocks Nick for a moment.

"What do you mean? I don't understand. My wife and I were under the impression that everything was fine. Shelley didn't mention that there were any hick-ups at work."

Jeff nods his head.

"Don't understand me wrong, mister Callahan; Shelley is a very good worker, and extremely good with the latest technological equipment. I don't know what the problem is, but it seems as if she loses interest after a while in what she is doing and then it's difficult for her to regain her focus."

Nick seconds this.

"Yes, I've noticed that Shelley's focus fades a little as time goes on. You mentioned that something happened here in the shop on Monday?"

"It's very odd. The man who came in here on Monday, is a young black man and has been here before. After he was here the first time, I asked Shelley who he was. She replied that he' was in the rehabilitation center with her. He spoke English with a very strong accent. I told Shelley that I didn't want him coming around to the shop, as he kept her out of her work. You can understand my surprise when he pitched up here on

Monday morning. Shelley was helping clients at the pay point when he arrived. He went straight to Shelley, where he placed a small plastic bag on the counter. Shelley saw him come in, and when he placed the bag on the counter, Shelley took it and placed it inside her bra. The man turned around and walked out. When my mother and I cornered her about the incident, Shelley lost her head."

Nick is about to make further enquiries, when his cell phone rings.

"Hello? Yes, this is Nick Callahan speaking. You've found Shelley? Where exactly? Oh, alright. Give me a couple of minutes; I'll be right there."

Nick excuses himself after the call.

"Thank you for the information, Jeff. Something has come up and I have to leave. We'll continue this conversation later on."

Nick departs hastily and drives away. A short time later, Nick drives around looking for the patrol car he is supposed to meet at a public park. Nick searches everywhere but can't find the patrol car. He is about to drive to the police station when he receives another call.

"Nick Callahan here. I'm on my way to the police station right this minute. Alright, I'll meet you there then."

The call is from the arresting officer. He decides to take Shelley to the police holding cells at the station, and asks Nick to meet him there. Nick arrives at the police station a few minutes before the patrol car pulls up.

Shelley rides in the back alone. Her hair is unkempt, and her clothing dirty and creased. Shelley doesn't look at Nick as she is escorted inside and put into the temporary holding cell. Nick tries to talk to Shelley, but to no avail.

A MINOR ADDICT

She refuses to answer any of Nick's questions and just keeps to herself. The youngster she is brought in with is also locked up in the cell with Shelley. Nick recognizes him as one of Shelley's previous drug-dependent friends.

155

CHAPTER TEN

Nick listens to what the arresting officer says to the youngster's mother, who starts crying when she sees her son. They have been found with narcotics in their possession, and are arrested immediately.

The arresting officer informs both Nick and the other boy's mother that they can see them at court the following morning. They will appear before a judge to determine whether they will be able to apply for bail.

Without any further ado, Nick leaves the police station and heads home. Arriving at his home a short time later, he informs Constance and Clark of all the latest developments. Constance is devastated when she hears about the incident on Monday morning, and even more so when she learns about the arrest due to possession.

"Nick, what do you think will happen in court tomorrow? Do you think Shelley would be allowed bail?"

"Oh yes, I'm sure Shelley will be asked whether she'd like to apply for bail, but I have a surprise for her. I'm not posting bail for her. Shelley can sit in jail until her next hearing in court, and I don't care how long it's for. It'll give her some time to rethink her values and goals in life and maybe, just maybe, give her some insight into what her life will be like if she carries on like this."

The horror on Constance's face at the hearing of Nick's words, makes him flinch. She doesn't expect to hear Nick say anything remotely close to what he's just said. Constance can't believe that Nick will say such a thing.

"B ..., but Nick, surely you don't mean that; I mean, not posting Shelley's bail? You can't just throw her to the wolves! She is our daughter, and we're the only way out she has. Please, Nick, if you don't want to do this for Shelley, do it for me."

"I'm sorry to disappoint you, my girl, but I am serious when I say that I'm not posting Shelley's bail. It's time she learnt a lesson or two. This might just save her life. She'll most probably cry and say bad things to us tomorrow, but she'll come round; you'll see."

Constance wipes the tears from her eyes.

"I hope you're right, Nick, because jail is an inhumane place to be."

Nick is adamant in his decision.

"She'll be alright; you'll see. Before you know it she's back home and driving you up the wall."

xxx

Friday, 19 July 2013. It's early-morning at the courthouse, and the passages are crammed with "not guilty" defendant's. They're ordinary folk from all walks-of-life, although today, they all have something in common; fighting the Judicial system.

Nick and Constance are also amongst those waiting for the court to begin its session. In the meantime, they try to see Shelley in the holding cells beneath the court, but aren't allowed down there before the court starts its proceedings.

Constance's nerves are shot, and she takes smoke breaks in short succession of one another. It's obvious that she did not have much sleep the previous night. Her eyes are baggy and bloodshot from loss of sleep.

A MINOR ADDICT

At last the court is called into session, and everybody files into Court, filling the gallery from the back. Nick and Constance sit right up front where the steps emerge from the bottom.

Shelley's hearing is first on the Court-roll, and when she appears at the top of the steps, she looks up and smiles at her parents. The smile is forced and stiff, and one can see the nervousness throb in the carotid artery of her neck.

Her face is chalk-white. She is still dressed in the same clothes she has been wearing since she has disappeared two days previously.

The proceedings don't take long. The Magistrate informs Shelley of the charges brought against her by the State, and asks whether she understands the charges. Shelley answers in a small voice that she does.

The magistrate then enquires from Shelley whether she has legal representation. Shelley shakes her head from side to side, indicating that she does not. Asking Shelley whether her parents are present in the court, she nods her head affirmatively. Shelley is asked to identify Nick and Constance. The Magistrate enquires from Nick whether he is going to post bail for Shelley, and Nick answers with a heavy heart.

"No, your Worship; I will not be posting bail for my daughter today."

The Magistrate looks from Shelley to Nick.

"You do realize of course, mister Callahan, that this leaves me no choice but to keep her incarcerated until her next hearing, or until such time when her bail is set forth?"

Nick nods his head.

"I understand, your Worship."

The Magistrate pounds with his gavel.

"Shelley Callahan, your next date to appear in court will be one week from today, on 26 July 2013. Bail was not posted for you, and you will be locked up until then. Bailiff, take Miss Callahan away."

The Bailiff takes Shelley by her arm and leads her towards the steps going down to the cells. Shelley cries and looks up as she passes her parents before descending the steps.

Constance asks the officer whether they can see Shelley before she is taken to prison. They are reluctantly given permission to speak to Shelley for a limited amount of time only.

At first Shelley doesn't want to speak to her parents, but realizes that she needs some clean clothing to take with her. She asks Constance for pajama's and a few other necessities, which Nick goes to purchase while Constance waits with Shelley. When Nick returns with Shelley's requested list, it's time to depart. Tears flow like a river.

A MINOR ADDICT

Tuesday, 23 July 2013. Nick finds out that visiting hours are from three o' clock to four o' clock on Tuesdays and Thursdays. He takes some time off from work and is on his way to visit Shelley in prison.

Constance says that she can't bear to see Shelley behind bars, and thus decides not to accompany Nick. Nick stops at a Kentucky Fried Chicken outlet and buys Shelley a variety of niceties, as he doesn't think that prison food is good to eat.

At the prison entrance as well as the entrance to the waiting area, the guards search the bag of goods. It takes some time before Shelley arrives. She cries when she enters the visitor's area and sees Nick waiting for her.

They are not allowed to make any physical contact. Nick has to find out from Shelley what exactly happened during the time she was unavailable. Shelley cries a lot more while she tells Nick what exactly happened.

"Daddy, I give you my word of honor that the drugs they found in my handbag, was not mine. I was standing outside the car smoking a cigarette when the police arrived on the scene. Michael saw the police coming, and had ample time to dump it in my handbag. Please daddy, I'm begging you; pay my bail on Friday. I'll kill myself if I have to stay here any longer. The other inmates have already taken all the new clothes you bought me, except these that I'm wearing. Please daddy!"

At that point Nick finds himself having regrets for not paying Shelley's bail money. He promises Shelley that him and Constance will be in court on Friday morning.

"Don't worry, honey; I'll post your bail on Friday, but I'm taking your cellphone to pay for your bail. You have a lot of numbers from drug-dealers on your phone. I'm going to destroy your sim card. I'll get you an Attorney as well to fight the case."

Visiting hour has passed, and Nick has to depart.

Shelley smiles when Nick leaves and thanks him numerous times. At least Nick can go home and give Constance the good news. She will be elated.

Time passes slowly for Constance, and she literally counts the hours until the morn of Friday. Nick hires a very good Attorney who immediately makes work of establishing Shelley's bail amount to a minimum.

Appearing in court is only a formality. The State Prosecutor doesn't protest Shelley's bail, and releases her into the custody of Nick and Constance, and another trial date is set. The attorney calls Nick to one side when they exit the courtroom.

"Mister Callahan, please don't forget to have Shelley here on the next trial date. If she doesn't appear in court on the said date, the judge will issue a warrant for her arrest, and you will forfeit the bail money. It's in your best interest to adhere to her bail conditions as well. Remember, Shelley may not leave the area without contacting the police, and she is to stay with you until such time that the case against her is solved. That's why she has been released into your custody."

They shake hands and Nick thanks Shelley's attorney.

"Thank you for all your help, mister Ludlow. We appreciate everything you've done so far."

Mister Ludlow smiles friendly.

"It's my pleasure, mister Callahan. Keep well; we'll speak again soon."

A MINOR ADDICT

xxx

Time goes by very quickly after that, with Shelley doing what she has always wanted to do; working with children. She meets a man quite a few years older than herself, and falls head over heels in love with him.

Nick and Constance organizes a barbeque so Shelley introduce them to her new boyfriend. Nick and Shelley's new boyfriend have met on a previous occasion, but not on good terms. Constance is afraid that the get-together will end in a disaster.

"Nick, please don't be rude or say something unnecessary. I don't want us to have a bad relationship with Shelley and her boyfriend. So whatever happens, please remain calm."

Nick has been watching Constance while she talks to him, and is once again struck by her unselfish attitude towards others. This is the reason why he fell in love with her, and will always love her, no matter what. He smiles as he draws her closer to hug her.

"It'll be alright, my girl; don't worry. I'll behave myself like a good gentleman should."

Constance smiles radiantly, encircling Nick's waist with her arms. She kisses him passionately on his mouth.

"Thank you, my knight in shining armor. I knew I could rely on you."

Just then, a car pulls up outside. Seeing that it's Shelley and her friend, Nick opens the gate. Shelley greets her parents before making the introductions.

"Daddy, mom, I'd like to introduce you to Arnold. Arnold, this is my dad, and this my mother."

Nick and Constance both shake Arnold's hand. After discussing trivial matters, Arnold and Shelley announce that there is a matter they'd like to address. Constance looks at Nick and nods her head, smiling at Shelley and Arnold. Nick has a premonition of what is about to come, and waits. Arnold clears his throat and drops the bomb.

"Mister and missus Callahan, I realize that we don't know each other at all. I would however, like to ask you for Shelley's hand in marriage. This might come as a surprise to you, but Shelley and I have known each other for quite some time now. I make a decent living and will look after her very well, I promise you."

Although Nick expects what is about to come, it still comes as a shock to him. When he looks over at Constance, he finds her smiling from ear to ear, her face glowing with excitement. She rushes to Shelley with stretched out arms and hugs her.

"Oh, my darling, that's just wonderful news! Arnold, welcome to the family. Nick, say something!"

Nick can't find the right words, and decides to speak his mind.

"Well, what do you expect me to say to that? It's not like anybody's about to listen to the grievances I have about this. Of course it's not alright! When do you two plan on getting married?"

There is a moment's hesitance. Arnold and Shelley look at one another before Arnold replies "Well, we'd like to get married as soon as possible, mister Callahan. We see no reason to wait too long."

Shelley has been quiet the whole time, but decides to stand her ground with Arnold.

"It's like Arnold says, daddy. There's no reason to wait that long. We'd like to get married in December."

Nick and Constance exchange puzzled looks. Nick can't believe what he's heard Shelley say just a moment before.

"What was that you just said, Shelley? You want to get married in December? I hope you mean December next year, because this year December is out of the question."

Shelley clears her throat before she continues.

"We actually meant this coming December, daddy."

Nick feels like a vein is going to pop in his head, and shakes his head while he retorts "It's three weeks from now! Do you realize how many things there are to plan? I don't think this is such a good idea. As a matter of fact, you should wait and get to know one another better before you make such a big decision."

Shelley quickly retaliates.

"Daddy, I don't want a big wedding, so don't worry about that; only a few friends and the closest family, that's it. We'll see to the catering for a small gathering afterwards."

Nick thinks about this for a couple of seconds and shrugs his shoulders. He knows that it will be of no use to try to put a stop to their plans. Shelley is twenty one and won't listen anyway, no matter what Nick says.

"Well, if that's the way you want to do things, I can't stop you. You're going to do as you please anyway."

Shelley's smile is brilliant as she hugs both Nick and Constance. Arnold shakes Nick's hand. "Thank you, daddy. We really appreciate your blessing in this regard."

Arnold also thanks Nick and Constance.

"Thank you both very much. This means a lot to us."

Nick is still not very happy with the turn of events, and is still unfriendly when he speaks.

"Hang on a minute. I never gave my blessing and I don't intend to either. You don't know him well enough, Shelley."

Shelley and Arnold stay for a while longer after the barbeque before they leave, with a promise to visit again soon. Constance is very happy that Shelley is going to be wed, as she can't wait to have grandchildren.

There is a huge argument between Nick and Arnold, and as a result Nick and Constance don't go to Shelley's wedding. It's a grave day for both parents, and a bitter pill to swallow. Nick has always dreamt of walking Shelley down the aisle in her wedding dress.

Constance has always wanted to help Shelley pick out her dress and prepare her for that wondrous day. Those dreams have been shattered in the blink of an eye.

Nick and Arnold never really find a common ground on which to communicate.

Shelley falls pregnant and gives birth to a beautiful little baby girl. Nick and Constance enjoy the little bundle of love with great enthusiasm.

Their little darling granddaughter is a ray of sunshine in both Nick's and Constance's lives. Nick isn't bothered by trivial little things as was his nature before. Constance can't survive the day without seeing her granddaughter for just five minutes.

Nick often thinks back to when Shelley was a toddler and the time her teens just started. She used to be "daddy's little girl", like his granddaughter now is. This brings a brilliant smile to Nick's lips as he remembers the good times they used to share. Clark is still Clark: happy with life.

THE END

167

Other hard drugs:

———

Following is a list of the most popular, strong drugs available in cities, where there is more money and the population is larger.

*ECSTASY:

Ecstasy is the Layman's term. (MDMA 3,4 methylenedioxymethamphetamine) is a synthetic, psychoactive drug chemically similar to the stimulant methamphetamine and the hallucinogen mescaline.

Street names for MDMA include:

1. Ecstasy
2. Adam
3. XTC
4. Hug drug
5. Beans
6. Love drug.

Ecstasy is an illegal drug that acts as both a stimulant and psychedelic, producing an energizing effect, as well as distortions in time and perception and enhanced enjoyment from tactile experiences.

Ecstasy exerts its primary effects in the brain on neurons that use the chemical serotonin to communicate with other neurons. The serotonin system plays an important role in regulating mood, aggression, sexual activity, sleep, and sensitivity to pain.

Ecstasy is neurotoxic. It can also be dangerous to health and, on rare occasions, lethal.

For some people, Ecstasy can be addictive. Almost 60 percent of people who use Ecstasy report withdrawal symptoms, including fatigue, loss of appetite, depressed feelings, and trouble concentrating.

Chronic users of Ecstasy perform more poorly than non-users on certain types of cognitive or memory tasks. Some of these effects may be due to the use of other drugs in combination with Ecstasy, among other factors.

In high doses, Ecstasy can interfere with the body's ability to regulate temperature. On rare occasions, this can lead to a sharp in-crease in body temperature (hyperthermia), resulting in liver, kidney, and cardiovascular system failure, and death.

Because Ecstasy can interfere with its own metabolism (breakdown within the body), potentially harmful levels can be reached by repeated drug use within short intervals.

Users of Ecstasy face many of the same risks as users of other stimulants such as cocaine and amphetamines. These include increases in heart rate and blood pressure, a special risk for people with circulatory problems or heart disease, and other symptoms such as muscle tension, involuntary teeth clenching, nausea, blurred vision, faintness, and chills or sweating.

Psychological Effects - These can include confusion, depression, sleep problems, drug craving, and severe anxiety. These problems occur during and for days or weeks after taking Ecstasy.

* COCAINE:

Cocaine, a powdered extract of the coca plant; it can be sniffed or smoked. When it is modified chemically for smoking, it is referred to as crack cocaine. Cocaine base is water soluble, while the crack form is not.

This means cocaine base can be dissolved in water, and injected or sniffed as powder into the nose. The lining of the nose and sinus cavity has enough water to dissolve the drug where it is absorbed into the blood stream.

Cocaine is extremely addictive, very damaging and difficult to break because the high is relatively short-lived. The effects of snorting cocaine usually fall off in about an hour, and another dose is required to maintain the high. This leads to repeated binge style administration of multiple doses.

Over time, the effect is to train the body to receive a regular supply of the drug. Cocaine, like other popular drugs, lives up to its reputation. It does cause euphoria and gives a sense of control. Sigmund Freud used cocaine. It makes shy people outgoing, increases conversational skills, and makes the fainthearted courageous.

These effects make the drug attractive to users whenever life presents problems. Of course, this is an illusion. No problem is actually solved and many new problems are introduced because of cocaine use. The repeated cycle of use and the positive reinforcement leads to more frequent use. The deadly cycle of addiction has started.

Cocaine addicts are 25% more likely to have a particular variant of a gene. This implies that risk of addiction increases depending on genetic makeup. It is not known exactly what these genes are responsible for, but it is assumed they impact the reward neurons in the brain.

Because cocaine affects the pleasure centers in the brain, repeated use begins to dull the normal ability to enjoy life without it. Repeated activation of reward neurons (dopamine and serotonin pathways) leads to physical changes in brain chemistry so that the 'cure' for feeling bad is to use more cocaine, more often. Snorting cocaine gives a quick, but temporary return to a better mood.

The alteration in brain chemistry often leads, over time, to cocaine induced paranoia and aggression. This mimics symptoms of schizophrenia and a common hallucination is the feeling of bugs crawling under the skin (cocaine bugs).

*Crystal Meth:

Is a strong central nervous system (CNS) stimulant that is mainly used as a recreational drug. In low doses, methamphetamine can cause an elevated mood and increase alertness, concentration, and energy in fatigued individuals. At higher doses, it can induce psychosis, rhabdomyolysis and cerebral hemorrhage.

Recreationally, methamphetamine's ability to increase energy has been reported to lift mood and increase sexual desire to an extent of users ability to engage in sexual activity continuously for several days.

It is of the phenethylamine and amphetamine classes. Methamphetamine has a high potential for recreational misuse and addiction. Heavy recreational use of methamphetamine may result in psychosis or lead to post-acute-withdrawal syndrome, a withdrawal syndrome that can persist for months beyond the typical withdrawal period. Unlike amphetamine, methamphetamine is neurotoxic to humans, damaging both dopamine and serotonin neurons in the CNS.

Contrary to the long-term use of amphetamine, there is evidence that methamphetamine causes brain damage from long-term use; this damage includes adverse changes in brain structure and function, such as reductions in grey matter volume in several brain regions and adverse changes in markers of metabolic integrity.

Methamphetamine is often used recreationally for its effects as a potent euphoriant and stimulant as well as aphrodisiac qualities. An entire subculture known as party and play is based around methamphetamine use.

A MINOR ADDICT

Members of this San Francisco sub-culture, which consists almost entirely of gay male methamphetamine users, meet up through internet dating sites and have sex. Due to its strong stimulant and aphrodisiac effects and inhibitory effect on ejaculation, with repeated use, these sexual encounters will sometimes occur continuously for several days on end.

The crash following the use of methamphetamine in this manner is very often severe, with marked hypersomnia (excessive daytime sleepiness).

<u>Methamphetamine is contra-indicated in individuals with</u>:

1. A history of substance use disorder
2. Heart disease
3. Severe agitation or anxiety

Or in individuals currently experiencing

1. Arteriosclerosis
2. Glaucoma
3. Hyperthyroidism
4. Severe hypertension.

<u>The physical effects of methamphetamine can include:</u>

1. Loss of appetite.
2. Hyperactivity.
3. Ddilated pupils.
4. Flushed skin.
5. Excessive sweating.
6. Increased movement.
7. Dry mouth.
8. Teeth grinding ("meth mouth").
9. Headache.

10. Irregular heartbeat (accelerated heartbeat or slowed heartbeat).
11. Rapid breathing.
12. High blood pressure.
13. Low blood pressure.
14. High body temperature.
15. Diarrhea.
16. Constipation.
17. Blurred vision.
18. Dizziness.
19. Twitching.
20. Numbness.
21. Tremors.
22. Dry skin.
23. Acne.
24. Pale appearance.

Methamphetamine that is present in a mother's bloodstream can pass through the placenta to a fetus and is secreted into breast milk. Infants born to methamphetamine-abusing mothers are found to have a significantly smaller gestational age-adjusted head circumference and birth weight measurements.

Methamphetamine exposure is also associated with neonatal withdrawal symptoms of agitation, vomiting and fast breathing. This withdrawal syndrome is relatively mild.

Methamphetamine users and addicts may lose their teeth abnormally quickly, regardless of the route of administration, from a condition informally known as meth mouth. The condition is generally most severe in users who inject the drug, rather than swallow, smoke, or inhale it.

Meth mouth is caused by a combination of drug-induced psychological and physiological changes resulting in a dry mouth, extended periods of poor oral hygiene, frequent consumption of high-calorie, carbonated beverages and teeth grinding and clenching.

Methamphetamine is related to higher frequencies of unprotected sexual intercourse in both HIV-positive and unknown casual partners, an association more pronounced in HIV-positive participants.

These findings suggest that methamphetamine use and engagement in unprotected anal intercourse are co-occurring risk behaviors that potentially heighten the risk of HIV transmission among gay and bisexual men. Methamphetamine use allows users of both sexes to engage in prolonged sexual activity, which may cause genital sores and abrasions as well as priapism in men. Methamphetamine may also cause sores and abrasions in the mouth via bruxism, increasing the risk of sexually transmitted infection.

Besides the sexual transmission of HIV, it may also be transmitted between users who share a common needle. The level of needle sharing among methamphetamine users is similar to that among other drug injection users.

The psychological effects of methamphetamine can include:

1. Euphoria
2. Dysphoria
3. Changes in libido
4. Alertness
5. Apprehension
6. Concentration
7. Decreased sense of fatigue
8. Insomnia or wakefulness
9. Self-confidence

10. Sociability
11. Irritability
12. Restlessness
13. Grandiosity and repetitive and obsessive behaviors.

<u>Methamphetamine use also has a high association with</u>:

1. Anxiety
2. Depression
3. Methamphetamine psychosis
4. Suicide
5. Violent behaviors.

A methamphetamine overdose may result in a wide range of symptoms.

<u>A moderate overdose of methamphetamine may induce symptoms such as</u>:

1. Abnormal heart rhythm
2. Confusion
3. Difficult and/or painful urination
4. High or low blood pressure
5. High body temperature
6. Over-active and/or over-responsive reflexes
7. Muscle aches
8. Severe agitation
9. Rapid breathing
10. Tremor
11. Urinary hesitancy
12. An inability to pass urine.

<u>An extremely large overdose may produce symptoms such as</u>:

1. Adrenergic storm
2. Methamphetamine psychosis
3. Substantially reduced or nil urine output
4. Cardiogenic shock
5. Brain bleed
6. Circulatory collapse
7. Dangerously high body temperature
8. Pulmonary hypertension
9. Kidney failure
10. Rhabdomyolysis
11. Serotonin syndrome
12. Form of stereotypy ("tweaking").

A methamphetamine overdose will likely also result in mild brain damage due to dopaminergic and serotonergic neurotoxicity. Death from methamphetamine poisoning is typically preceded by convulsions and coma.

Tolerance is expected to develop with regular methamphetamine use and, when used recreationally, this tolerance develops rapidly. In dependent users, withdrawal symptoms are positively correlated with the level of drug tolerance. Depression from methamphetamine withdrawal lasts longer and is more severe than that of cocaine withdrawal.

Withdrawal symptoms in chronic, high-dose users are frequent, and persist for three to four weeks with a marked "crash" phase occurring during the first week. <u>Methamphetamine withdrawal symptoms can include</u>:

1. Anxiety.
2. Drug craving.
3. Dysphoric mood.

4. Fatigue.
5. Increased appetite.
6. Increased movement or decreased movement.
7. Lack of motivation.
8. Sleeplessness or sleepiness.
9. Vivid or lucid dreams.

<u>* MANDRAX:</u>

Mandrax was initially marketed as a sedative or sleeping tablet in the beginning. <u>Mandrax tablets are also known as:</u>

1. Buttons
2. Whites.
3. Mandies.

Mandrax was originally a white tablet with the words Mx written on it. These days, because they are produced illegally and because of additives, they are sometimes grey or yellow in color.

Mandrax is still sold illegally in South Africa. In conjunction with Marijuana(Weed), it is the most widely used drug of choice in the Western Cape. In fact, Cape Town is reportedly seen as the Mandrax capital of the world.

It appears to be the drug of choice in the ganglands of the Cape Flats. Mandrax retails at approximately R30–35 per tablet, but re-cently the quality seems to be depreciating, forcing users to buy larger quantities in order to achieve the same high as five years ago.

Mandrax can be swallowed or injected, but is usually smoked. The tablets are usually crushed and mixed with dagga and then smoked using a pipe or a bottleneck. This pipe is also known as a 'white pipe'.

Minutes after smoking Mandrax, the user will feel relaxed, calm and peaceful and everything will feel perfect. Some people will feel aggressive as the effects start wearing off.

The effects last for several hours where the user will have a dry mouth and very little appetite. Others have slurred speech and stumble or stagger.

Nausea, vomiting and stomach pains are not unusual. A user will often have red, glazed or puffy eyes, especially if the Mandrax is taken together with Marijuana.

Increased usage in order to achieve the same effects as before is usually the first sign of a full scale addiction developing. In many cases, users feel tired after taking Mandrax and may go to sleep for lengthy periods. Depression is also not uncommon and is part and parcel of the Mandrax 'hangover'. This often leads to repeated use of Mandrax to counteract the negative and unpleasant feelings.

<u>Withdrawal from Mandrax takes place a few days after stopping use</u>:

1. Sleeping problems.
2. Nervous.
3. Anxious and irritable feelings.
4. Headaches.
5. Restlessness and eating problems are also common.

Mandrax has proven to be a particularly difficult habit to break.

Cocaine, LSD(Acid) and Ecstasy are also amongst the more expensive drugs, but very easily obtainable.

Nyaope is not as expensive, although it is a mixture of some of the most potent drugs around. The reason for this is that the dealers mix small amounts of strong drugs with dangerous chemicals such as pool cleaner, rat poison (even ant poison) and other lethal chemicals.

Dealers are very slippery as they have found ways to disperse of their products in a quick and efficient way without being caught. They are caught eventually when someone, usually a client or user, contacts the police to sell them out.

The reason for this might be or are in many instances because the person wants to break the habit of taking drugs any longer. This person then becomes an informant, supplying the police with inside information that helps them obtain search warrants to carry out a drug bust.

While an informant is sometimes an integral part of the chain in combatting the drug trade, he or she may not be on drugs. They are warned by the narcotics squad that it is a crime to take drugs, and should they be found with drugs in their possession, they will be prosecuted as well.

When a drug bust is orchestrated, it is done in conjunction with the local Canine unit, or in some cases, a central Canine unit from the city.

The Canine's(dogs) are sent in with their respective handlers to sniff the property which is suspected of housing drugs, and find the drugs in a much shorter time, as the police do not always know where the drugs are stashed. Canine's noses are very sensitive to the strong smell of drugs, and they therefor very seldom make mistakes.

When caught with drugs in one's possession, the sentencing for such a crime depends on a number of circumstances. The person charged with the crime stands trial, and depending on whether or not he or she is a first time offender, the amount and value of the drugs are taken into consideration.

A sentence is then passed down to the offender. It can be said with all honesty that drug dealers never get a sentence that fits the crime. The time they serve behind bars is not adequate enough, as no-one can put a price on the life of another innocent human being.

181

CLAY CASSIDY

ABOUT THE AUTHOR

Clay Cassidy was born in a small town in South Africa in 1963. Clay has alwaysbeen an avid reader since early childhood, as well as a very keen writer at a young age. Clay is well-known in the Western genre for his unique writing style and stories about the Wild West. Apart from writing novels, Leonard is also a very good artist, and busies himself with oil paintings and pencil sketching.

Clay also Edits, Proofreads and formats manuscripts for aspiring writers as well as famous novelists. Clay also does cover designing.

Did you love *A Minor Addict*? Then you should read *A Dish Best Served Cold*[1] by Clay Cassidy!

[2]

Because he was a Sheriff and laid down rules, they killed his wife and child in cold blood; burnt his home to the ground. The only way he could deal with it, was to avenge his wife and child's inexcusable deaths.

---

1. https://books2read.com/u/mVXQRM

2. https://books2read.com/u/mVXQRM

Also by Clay Cassidy

Payback
The Judge
The Return
The Serial Killer
A Dozen Lawmen
Wrong Diagnosis
Rebel Cowgirl
A Minor Addict
A Dish Best Served Cold

www.ingramcontent.com/pod-product-compliance
Lightning Source LLC
Chambersburg PA
CBHW071321140726
47996CB00005B/1759